# A Lenten Journey with Mother Mary

FR. EDWARD LOONEY

# A
# LENTEN JOURNEY
# WITH
# MOTHER MARY

SOPHIA INSTITUTE PRESS
Manchester, New Hampshire

Sophia Institute Press
Box 5284, Manchester, NH 03108
1-800-888-9344

www.SophiaInstitute.com

Sophia Institute Press® is a registered trademark of Sophia Institute.

**Library of Congress Cataloging-in-Publication Data**

Names: Looney, Edward, author.
Title: A Lenten journey with Mother Mary / Fr. Edward Looney.
Description: Manchester, New Hampshire : Sophia Institute Press, 2020.
Summary: "A collection of meditations and prayers, with a Marian theme, for each day of Lent and the Easter Octave"— Provided by publisher.
Identifiers: LCCN 2019041880  ISBN 9781622828487 (paperback)  ISBN 9781622828494 (ebook)
Subjects: LCSH: Mary, Blessed Virgin, Saint—Prayers and devotions.  Mary, Blessed Virgin, Saint—Devotion to.  Lent—Prayers and devotions.
Classification: LCC BX2160.23 .L665 2020  DDC 242/.34—dc23
LC record available at https://lccn.loc.gov/2019041880

First printing

# Contents

First Week of Lent
## Examining Your Conscience

Second Week of Lent
## Praying for Others

Third Week of Lent
## Intentional Prayer Continued

Fourth Week of Lent
## Mary Teaches Us Methods of Prayer

### Fifth Week of Lent
## Healing

## Holy Week

## Easter Octave

# Introduction

Lourdes, a village in the Pyrenees Mountains of France, is one of my favorite places in the world to pray. It was there, in 1858, that the Blessed Virgin appeared to St. Bernadette Soubirous, transforming a garbage dump into a beautiful grotto for Our Lady. Every time I sit in front of the grotto and pray, I sense the love of Mary. Gazing up at the Madonna of the grotto, I am caught up in the beauty of the Blessed Virgin, the Immaculate Conception.

On the last day of one of my many visits to Lourdes, I found myself at one of my favorite restaurants in town. I had just finished my meal when another American walked in to dine. While in Lourdes, whenever I hear someone speak English, my ears perk up, and typically I start a conversation with the person. This was true for the American who just walked in. Let's call her Anna.

I was wearing my Green Bay Packers fleece jacket with pride. As Anna passed by my table, she shared that she was from Chicago, whose football team is one of the archrivals of the Green Bay Packers. I asked her if this was her first time in Lourdes, and it was. She joined me at my table and ordered her meal, and I began to tell her what she must do during her three days there. Whenever I talk to someone in Lourdes, I ask the person, "What brought you here?" It is a place known for healing. And the stories of people find a way into my heart and my prayer. What Anna shared was a beautiful spiritual story detailing her European journey. She traveled alone, as I do, and Lourdes was neither her first destination nor her last.

Anna had been in a difficult marriage , and after only a short while, she and her husband separated. This led her on a spiritual journey of prayer, retreat, pilgrimage, and healing. She traveled a lot for work and had amassed frequent-flyer miles and hotel points, and at some point, she decided she needed to make a religious pilgrimage to Europe. It was not going to be like any pilgrimage you or I have ever taken. She wanted to spend a few months on this journey. She had a plan and a reason for all of it, and she also relied on divine providence to guide her.

The first leg of her trip was to complete what is called *El Camino de Santiago*, or the Way of St. James. This is a pilgrim's journey on foot, beginning in Spain, France, or Portugal, to the town of Compostela, in Spain. During these days of walking, a person experiences a lot—physically, mentally, emotionally, and spiritually. Anna wanted to walk the Way of St. James so she could let go of a lot of anger and hurt. A person walks the *Camino* with all his belongings in a backpack. Along the way, he might have to let go of something to make the bag lighter and easier to carry.

After she completed the *Camino*, Anna headed to Fatima, Portugal, the site of a series of Marian apparitions received by three children in 1917. Our Lady, in her messages there, encouraged the recitation of the Rosary and taught the children some additional prayers, one being what is called the Fatima prayer, often added to the end of each decade of the Rosary: "O my Jesus, forgive us our sins, save us from the fires of hell; lead all souls to Heaven, especially those who have most need of Your mercy." Anna said she went to Fatima because she was looking for forgiveness. It seemed like a natural progression: after she spent some time letting go of her emotional and spiritual baggage, she wanted to seek the Lord's mercy. She believed Fatima was the place for that.

From Fatima, she headed to Lourdes, where she sat across from me in the restaurant. Many physical healings have happened at Lourdes, but spiritual and emotional healings happen as well. In Lourdes, people immerse themselves in the *piscines*, or baths, and wash themselves in the healing water discovered by St. Bernadette in 1858. Anna was seeking the healing of her soul, her heart, and also seeking healing from a physical infirmity from which she suffered.

Anna told me that she planned to visit Poland next, especially the Shrine of Divine Mercy. In the 1920s, Jesus began appearing and speaking to St. Faustina. These experiences are recorded in her diary, *Divine Mercy in My Soul*. The popular image of Divine Mercy, of Jesus with red and white rays coming forth from His heart, has the words "Jesus, I Trust in You" at the bottom. For Anna, after she let everything go, sought forgiveness, and prayed for healing, she wanted to develop a greater trust in God.

I share Anna's story because I was privileged to be a part of it and to share in it. Her sharing her faith in God, manifested through pilgrimage, touched my soul. I hope and pray that Anna received what she sought on her European pilgrimage. I also share her story because I think it is the movement of our hearts and spiritual lives during Lent. Our meditations in these pages, spanning the season of Lent, will be a journey similar to Anna's.

# A Lenten Journey with Mother Mary

In the first week, we will let go of our sins as we examine our consciences and later seek forgiveness through the sacrament of Reconciliation. In weeks two and three, we will respond to Our Lady's request to pray for specific intentions, focusing on one each day. In our fourth week, we will learn different methods of prayer and give each a try, and in the fifth, we will focus on the need for healing in our lives and in our world. During the Triduum—Holy Thursday, Good Friday, and Holy Saturday—we will move to a reflection about Mary in those days of Jesus' life. During the Easter Octave, we will continue with a postlude to our Lenten journey and turn our focus to St. Faustina, just as Anna ended her pilgrimage to Poland and the Shrine of Divine Mercy. During these days we will focus on developing greater trust in God.

# How to Use This Book

It might seem a little silly to provide a few thoughts about how to use this book. After all, it is straightforward; it is a Lenten meditation book, similar to other devotionals I'm sure you've used. I've been in your shoes: I've been excited to get a book I wanted to pray with during Advent or Lent, but then I quickly fell behind and was not sure what to do next.

If this happens to you, don't become discouraged. While it is ideal to read all the meditations, so as to understand better Mary's messages at approved apparitions, don't let falling behind cause you to leave the book on the nightstand until next year. If you have fallen three or four days behind, get back on track by reading the reflection for the given day. If you feel so inclined, read one of the meditations you missed, either at the same time, or maybe at another spare moment, or before bed. If you miss an entire week, that's okay. Begin again, starting with the week you are currently in. The devil wants to discourage us and does not want us to draw closer to God in prayer. The devil doesn't want us to listen to Mary, because her foot is the one that will crush the serpent's ugly head.

# A Lenten Journey with Mother Mary

Although this book is billed as a Lenten devotional, the meditations, aside from those of Holy Week, which are specific to that time, can be a source of prayer, reflection, and action anytime during the year, perhaps when we need to hit the reset button and refocus on our spiritual lives.

Ash Wednesday

# Mary Prays for Us

*"I am the Queen of Heaven, who prays*
*for the conversion of sinners."*

—Our Lady in Champion, Wisconsin

Today begins our Lenten journey. Even though it's not a holy day of obligation, many people go to church to commence this yearly observance. We are marked with ashes, a reminder of our death. We are invited to pray more this Lent, perhaps with the Stations of the Cross. We decide to make small sacrifices, acts of denial, to suffer just a little as a reminder of the suffering of Christ. Some people hope for a life-altering season as they give up vices and bad habits, such as overconsumption of caffeine, alcohol, or sweets. For some, those little penances offered to God become the grace they receive on Easter Sunday, as they continue to deny themselves after the penitential season.

Lent is a time to take our spiritual lives more seriously—to read, pray, and meditate. I hope this book will help you to do just that.

Over the next several weeks, we will journey with the Blessed Virgin Mary and ponder the many messages she spoke to children and adults throughout the years. The Lenten themes of prayer, penance, and conversion are the same themes that the Mother of God addressed in her apparitions over the last several centuries. We will meet the visionaries and apply the messages of Mary to our daily lives and our Lenten observances.

There is one apparition that holds a special place in my heart. It took place in 1859 in the Diocese of Green Bay, the diocese where I was born, raised, and now serve as a Catholic priest. The Blessed Virgin appeared to Adele Brise, a twenty-eight-year-old Belgian immigrant. After seeing the silent, beautiful woman twice, Adele asked the local priest what she should do. He instructed her to ask the woman who she was and what she wanted. That's what Adele did when she saw the Virgin for the third time. "In God's name, who are you, and what do you want of me?" she asked. Mary responded, "I am the Queen of Heaven, who prays for the conversion of sinners." So Adele learned not only her identity, but, even more special, that the Queen of Heaven was praying for her. Adele was a sinner. You are a sinner. I am a sinner. The great news is that we have an intercessor in Heaven who is praying for us. We ask her so often to do that: *Pray for us sinners now and at the hour of our death.* Yes, Mary prays for us sinners, but even more specifically, she is praying for our conversion.

As we begin this season of Lent, a season calling us to conversion of life, we know that Mary prays for us. Even as we begin our Lenten observance, as we hunger through fasting, as we struggle to find time to pray, we should be at peace, because Mary is praying for us. During the next several weeks, don't forget that. Remind yourself often that Mary is praying for you. Even if we forget to ask, she prays for us; she will not forget her children.

*Dear Blessed Mother, whisper my name in Jesus' ear and ask Him to help me live this Lent to the fullest. Through your intercession, obtain for me the grace of conversion where I need it most.*

## Lenten Action

Spend a few moments in prayer today and consider what aspect of your life needs greatest conversion. In what area of your life have you not conformed to Christ or heeded His teaching? Make a resolution to strive to turn toward the Lord.

Thursday after Ash Wednesday

# Queen of Prophets

*In times past, God spoke in partial and various ways to*
*our ancestors through the prophets; in these last days,*
*he spoke to us through a son, whom he made heir of all*
*things and through whom he created the universe.*

—Hebrews 1:1–2

The Old Testament contains many allusions to Mary and Jesus. Some Scripture scholars contend that one should not read Marian imagery into prophetic texts because that was not the intention of the author. Yet we see these Scripture passages fulfilled with Jesus and Mary. For example, Isaiah prophesied about a virgin being with child. Mary is a perpetual virgin—before, during, and after the birth of Christ. Genesis says that the woman's foot would crush the head of the serpent (3:15). Mary, as the New Eve, fulfills that, and our art depicts her as such; for example, in the statue of Our Lady of Grace.

The prophets called people back to God. God spoke His word through the prophets to a wayward people. The messages of Mary's apparitions speak to us today about conversion of life. When people have fallen away from the sacraments of Penance and the Eucharist, Our Lady comes to invite people back to sacramental participation. In times of war and disturbance, she urges us to pray for peace. In some of her apparitions, she even prophesied about future events, as in Kibeho, Rwanda, when she said a river of blood would flow throughout the country; the Rwandan genocide occurred a few years later. In Fatima, she said a worse war would break out after World War I, which was being fought at the time.

I often analogize the seasons of Advent and Lent to our lives: Advent because we are awaiting the Lord's return in glory; Lent because, preparing to celebrate the Paschal Mystery of Jesus' life, death, and Resurrection helps us to anticipate our own resurrected life. Soon, our Lenten meditations will intensify as we focus on Mary's message. As we consider the prophetic utterances related to Jesus and Mary, knowing that they pertained to Christ as our Savior, it will do us good to ponder our need for Jesus' saving work.

*Dear Mary, thank you for saying yes to bearing Christ so that He might die for me. During this Lenten season, help me to hear your message and know why I need a Savior and how I can grow in relationship with Him.*

### Lenten Action

Spend time asking Mary to crush the serpent's ugly head in your life. Ask her to show you how virtue can help root out vice.

# Evaluating Apparitions

*By their fruits you will know them.*

—Matthew 7:16

You might hear people talk about going on religious pilgrimages. Sometimes people go on pilgrimages to Rome or to the Holy Land. Many people travel to France, Spain, and Portugal and visit the various sites of Marian apparitions, such as Lourdes, Rue du Bac, or Fatima. This Lent, we are on a spiritual pilgrimage together. We won't physically visit all these sites, but spiritually we will listen to Mary's voice and her message. We will meet the visionaries and learn their stories and what they mean for our lives.

It is important to note that we do not treat these Marian apparitions as we do Scripture. The Church uses specific language in this regard. For example, Scripture consists of what is called public revelation, whereas apparitions are private revelation. Although we are required to believe in the content of public revelation, we need not believe what is contained in the messages received in private revelations. When Bishop Ricken approved the 1859 apparitions received by Adele Brise, in his decree of approval he stated that the apparitions were worthy of belief, though not obligatory for the Christian faithful. The reality is that those who follow the apparitions find a source of spiritual strength and renewal from the messages. The messages confront them to live better and holier lives.

How does an apparition get judged as worthy of belief? The Vatican's Congregation for the Doctrine of the Faith released a document on the norms for evaluating an apparition. There are both positive and negative factors to consider, such as the life of the visionary, the content of the message, and the spiritual fruit the apparition bears after it occurs. After a formal process of inquiry, the local bishop can make a judgment regarding the veracity of the claims, as the bishop of Green Bay did in 2010.

This Lenten pilgrimage will introduce you to many of the popular apparitions and also to some of the more obscure ones. Through it you will hear Mary' voice and begin to see how she speaks to your heart. She has come as a mother to us on earth, and in her messages, you will discover her motherly concern.

*Dear Blessed Mother, please pray for me that I might be open to all the graces God wants to give me during this Lent. Help me to respond to your messages and live them in my life.*

### Lenten Action

Which Marian apparitions do you know about? Consider making a list and seeing if you know the basic message of each apparition. Then ask yourself: How do I live Our Lady's message?

Saturday after Ash Wednesday

# Listen to Your Mother

*"Know and understand well, you the most humble of*
*my sons, that I am the ever-virgin Holy Mary, Mother*
*of the True God, for whom we live, of the Creator*
*of all things, Lord of heaven and the earth."*

—Our Lady of Guadalupe

Jesus listened to Mary throughout His childhood. We hear this
in Luke's Gospel when Jesus' parents find Him in the Temple.
His parents ask a question. Jesus listens and responds. Then we
are told that He returns to Nazareth and is obedient to Mary
and Joseph, learning from them and growing in age and wisdom
(see Luke 2:41–52).

Mary is our mother too. And she teaches us. Just as Jesus
listened to and was obedient to Mary, we should now listen to
and obey her. Through many apparitions, Our Lady has spoken
to various visionaries and imparted her motherly advice and
counsel, not only for them but for the entire world. The messages
Mary spoke are meant for all believers.

The counsel our mothers gave us was always meant for our
good. Sometimes what they told us we already knew. Other
things we didn't want to hear because they were difficult and

challenging. And maybe, years later, we look back and are grateful for our mothers' advice. The same is true about Mary's apparitions and messages. Sometimes she challenges us and tells us things we don't want to hear, but she does so for our benefit. We will encounter many messages throughout our Lenten pilgrimage. Here are a few things to know about each of Mary's apparitions:

*Guadalupe*: The Virgin of Guadalupe appeared to Juan Diego in December 1531. She taught Juan Diego that she was the Mother of the true, living God and instructed him to go to the bishop and ask for a church to be built. The bishop requested a sign, and Our Lady showed Juan where to find roses, miraculously growing in the winter, which he gathered and brought to the bishop, unveiling the miraculous image of Our Lady still venerated by pilgrims today.

*Laus, France*: In this series of apparitions, received over several decades (1664–1718) by Benoîte Rencurel , Mary is honored under the title Refuge of Sinners. Her message here focused on conversion of life, emphasizing respect for God's name. The apparitions received Church approval on May 5, 2008.

*Rue du Bac, France*: Our Lady appeared to St. Catherine Laboure here in 1830. During these apparitions, Our Lady requested the creation of the Miraculous Medal, bearing the words "O Mary, conceived without sin, pray for us who have recourse to thee."

*La Salette, France*: Two children in the French Alps, Maximin and Melanie, along with their dog, witnessed three stages of Mary's appearance on September 19, 1846. A popular image associated with the apparition is Our Lady, in a sitting posture, with her face in her hands, crying. Mary spoke about sorrow for sin, especially regarding the Lord's name and keeping holy the Sabbath.

*Lourdes, France*: The young St. Bernadette Soubirous happened to go with her sisters to collect wood on a fateful day in 1858 and received the first of eighteen apparitions of Our Lady. Mary identified herself as the Immaculate Conception and encouraged Bernadette to do penance for sinners. A healing spring of water was discovered, and, to this day, pilgrims drink and bathe in the healing waters.

*Champion, Wisconsin*: In 1859, the Belgian immigrant Adele Brise received three apparitions of the Queen of Heaven. The first two were silent apparitions. During the final apparition, Adele received her marching orders to pray for the conversion of sinners, especially by offering her Holy Communions for that intention and gathering the children and teaching them what they needed to know for salvation.

*Pontmain, France*: Our Lady appeared on January 17, 1871, during the Franco-Prussian War , revealing herself only to children gathered in the area. The apparition had three phases, and in the final phase, the words "But pray, my children. God will hear you in time. My Son allows Himself to be touched" appeared in the sky above Our Lady, who was dressed in blue, with stars on her dress, and wearing a crown. In this apparition, Mary is honored under the title Our Lady of Hope.

*Knock, Ireland*: On August 21, 1879, about twenty-five people witnessed the silent apparition of Our Lady, accompanied by St. Joseph, St. John, and a lamb on the altar. The apparition lasted nearly two hours.

*Fatima, Portugal*: Three shepherd children, Francisco, Jacinta, and Lucia, received a series of apparitions. In 1916, they were visited by the Angel of Portugal, who prepared them for the 1917 Marian apparitions on the thirteenth of each month, from May through October, with the exception of August, when the children were imprisoned. Our Lady requested the daily recitation of the Rosary and desired peace in the world. She revealed three secrets to the children and allowed them to see Hell. On October 13, 1917, Mary told the children that she was Our Lady of the Holy Rosary and revealed herself also as the Sorrowful Mother and Our Lady of Mount Carmel. St. Joseph with the Christ Child appeared beside the Blessed Mother.

*Beauraing, Belgium*: Our Lady appeared a total of thirty-three times to three Voisin children and two Degeimbre children. The first apparition occurred on November 29, 1932, and the last one took place on January 3, 1933. Mary encouraged the children to pray often and be good. During the apparition, Our Lady identified herself with a few traditional titles, such as the Immaculate Virgin, and she revealed her golden heart, making the apparition better known as Our Lady of the Golden Heart.

*Banneux, Belgium*: The appellation of Mary associated with the apparitions in Banneux is Our Lady of the Poor. Mary appeared to a young girl name Mariette Beco. The first apparition was on January 15, 1933, on the heels of the Beauraing apparition. Many people believed Mariette was just imitating what happened in Beauraing and did not take her seriously. Mary showed Mariette the way to a spring of water (one that already existed) and told her that through the spring she would relieve suffering. The final apparition took place on March 2, 1933.

*Kibeho, South Rwanda*: Rwandan genocide survivor, author, and popular speaker Immaculée Ilibagiza popularized these apparitions through her devotion and authorship of a book retelling the accounts of the happenings, in addition to a devotional on the Seven Sorrows Rosary. The apparitions occurred in 1981 and prophesied the forthcoming Rwandan genocide if hearts did not change.

There are other apparitions I have chosen not to include, because, although it seems that the Church has approved them, I thought that the controversies that surround them might distract us from our pilgrimage. Examples of these apparitions are Akita, Our Lady of Good Success, Our Lady of All Nations, Our Lady of America, and the San Nicholas apparitions. The status of Medjugorje is quite complicated, and although Medjugorje is popular among many devotees of private revelation, it has been omitted from this book.

Together we are on a pilgrimage this Lent. We will meet Our Lady and listen to her words. She has the best advice for us. Let's listen and live it in our lives.

*Mother Mary, during this Lenten pilgrimage, help me to listen to your words and motherly counsel and, in so doing, realize how much you love me and want what is best for me.*

## Lenten Action

Think about your childhood and all the many things your parents taught you. Is there one thing your mother said, or an instruction or counsel she gave, that you cling to even to this very day? Spend a few moments thanking God for your mother, for the gift of life, for her love and concern. You might even wish to call your mother today and check in with her and tell her that you were thinking about her. Or, if she has passed on to eternal life, offer a prayer for her soul.

First Week of Lent

# Examining Your Conscience

Our Lady's messages throughout the years often invite us back
into a relationship with God when we have gone astray. Following the model of Anna's pilgrimage, in which she had to let go
of certain things and find forgiveness, this week we will examine
our consciences to notice the areas of our lives where we might
need growth or conversion.

# How Mary Converts Sinners

*"I will convert sinners."*

—Our Lady of Beauraing

When Mary spoke to Gilberte Voison, one of the children of Beauraing to whom she appeared, she made a very bold and emphatic statement: "I will convert sinners." For me, this raised a question that became a topic of prayer, reflection, and meditation. I asked, "How does she do it? How does Mary convert sinners?" These are a few answers I came up with.

## By Her Presence

The very theme of our Lenten meditation, the messages spoke in her many apparitions, become a source of conversion for those who listen to and live the messages. Mary's presence in the world, speaking messages, in most cases, to children, but on occasion to adults, facilitates the conversion of sinners. In Guadalupe, Our Lady appeared to Juan Diego, and in the years that followed, many people were baptized. Other individuals have heard the message of Mary, and it completely transformed their lives. Alphonse Ratisbonne was a skeptic about the Miraculous

Medal but ended up converting to the Faith and becoming a Catholic priest. One way Mary converts sinners is through her presence and through the messages she speaks because of her concern for God's wayward children.

## By Her Prayers

As we reflected on Ash Wednesday, Mary prays for the conversion of sinners. This is her role as the Queen Mother; she advocates before the throne of her Son for the world and all people, sinners that we are. Mary becomes grieved by our sins and, seeing them, pleads for our conversion. Many a sinner has been converted by her prayers and our prayers joined to hers.

## By Her Example

We meet the Blessed Virgin in the pages of the Gospel. The way she lived her life offers us a great example. When we are confronted with vices, we look to Mary's virtues. When we are tempted toward pride, we remember her humility before God. When we want to be disobedient, we recall her obedience to God's will. When impurity and unchastity confront us, her example of purity and chastity inspires us to live similarly. When we wish to ignore the needs of our brothers and sister in Christ, her attentiveness and generosity toward Elizabeth beckon us to respond to others' needs.

> *Mary, my mother, please pray for me, that I may know the areas in my life where God is inviting me to conversion. As I reflect on your role in salvation history, especially through the Rosary, allow me to know your virtues; and pray for me, that I might put them into practice in my life.*

## Lenten Action

Open your Bible today and read chapters 1 and 2 of Luke. Then pray about this question: "How does Mary's example in the Scriptures invite me to conversion in my life?" What do you admire about Mary's response to God and her interaction with others? This week, try to find moments to live like Mary, growing in that virtue you found in her example.

Monday of the First Week of Lent

# Purity

*"I am the Immaculate Conception."*
—Our Lady of Lourdes

During the summer months, youth from all over the world attend large Catholic youth conferences. They listen to speakers, pray together, attend Mass, and go home renewed to serve the Lord. Often, the young men and women will break into groups and listen to speakers address a very important topic, that of purity. Purity, when spoken about in this context, refers to chastity and sexuality. St. Thomas Aquinas, in his treatise on theology, the *Summa Theologica*, describes purity in this sense. Even Our Lady in her apparitions to the children of Fatima, spoke about the gravity of sexual sins, saying that more souls go to Hell because of sins of the flesh than because of any other sin. When Our Lady spoke to St. Bernadette and identified herself as the "Immaculate Conception," she revealed to us a greater depth of purity in virtue of her Immaculate Conception.

What does it mean for Mary to be without sin? It means that she was spared the taint and consequences of original sin, the sin of our first parents in the Garden of Eden. Mary did not suffer any concupiscence—that is, an inclination to sin. Everything in her life was motivated by a pure love of God and neighbor. Mary's Immaculate Conception invites us to a greater depth of purity in mind, body, heart, and soul.

Purity of mind refers to thinking good, godly thoughts. An impure mind fixates on negative, evil thoughts. A pure mind thinks good of others, even if it means making excuses for them.

Purity of heart focuses on intention. Do I do a kind act for someone so that he will do something for me in the future? If so, my intention is to do good so that someone will owe me a favor. Purity of heart has no such selfish ambition.

Purity of body means that we live according to our vocations in life. This purity encompasses our thoughts and, more importantly, our actions. Purity of body requires practicing self-restraint.

Purity of soul pertains to our sins. Mary is the model Christian disciple. She was without sin, so she gives us an example to strive for. When we fall to temptations against charity or chastity, or any other sins, let us seek out the sacrament of Reconciliation. When we receive that sacrament, God restores us to the original innocence He intended for all of us.

Mary gives us an example of purity. She lived with purity of mind, as she singularly devoted herself to God at a very young age, thinking holy and pious thoughts. She had a purity of heart, because after she received the news of salvation from the angel, she declared her *fiat*, "let it be done unto me," signifying that she wanted only what God wanted for her life. She knew purity of body, as she asked the angel, "How can this be since I have no relations with a man?" (Luke 1:34). Because of God's preservation of Mary from original sin by the Immaculate Conception, Mary shines forth as pure in soul. During these days of Lent, and really every day of our lives, let us look to Mary as an example of what it means to live purely.

Mary, the Immaculate Conception, pray for me that live purely in mind, body, heart, and soul.

## Lenten Action

As you go about your day today, take a few moments at lunch and on your drive home to think about your actions throughout the day. What were your motivations for your actions? In the evening, do an examination of conscience, asking these questions: Were my thoughts today pure? Were my actions pure? Was I pure in my interactions with those of the opposite sex?

# The Lord's Day

*"Only a few rather old women go to Mass in the summer.*
*Everyone else works every Sunday all summer long.*
*And in the winter, when they don't know what else to*
*do, they go to Mass only to scoff at religion. During*
*Lent, they go to the butcher shops like dogs."*

—Our Lady of La Salette

Once, when I was on a pilgrimage in Europe, our tour guide told us that we should wait until after Sunday to do our shopping. On Sunday, she told us to notice which stores were closed. She encouraged us to patronize them and support their business because they understood the nature of religious tourism and the value of worship. The same can be said for stores such as Hobby Lobby and restaurants such as Chick-fil-A, which close on Sundays so their employees can spend time with their families, but most importantly, so that they can go to church.

Lent is a good time for us to examine our commitment to Sunday Mass. Have you missed Mass recently? What was the reason? Was it because of illness or hazardous weather conditions? If so, then you are in the clear. If those weren't your reasons, then what was more important than Sunday Mass? A sporting event? Some other commitment?

The *Catechism of the Catholic Church* teaches about the severity of missing Mass, classifying it as a mortal sin (see CCC 2180–2183). That means that a person who, without good reason, has missed Mass on a Sunday or on a holy day of obligation should avail himself of the sacrament of Reconciliation before receiving Holy Communion.

Why is missing Sunday Mass such a big deal? First, because God commanded us to keep holy the Lord's Day. For the Jewish people, the Sabbath was observed on Saturday. But for Christians, the Lord's Day became the day of Resurrection—Sunday. The early Christians gathered in the early hours of Sunday, the first day of the week, and sang hymns and broke bread together. When we skip Sunday Mass, we break God's commandment, but more importantly, we deprive ourselves of the gift of the Eucharist. If we truly believe that the Eucharist is the Body, Blood, Soul, and Divinity of Jesus, that He makes His home within us at every Holy Communion, then we should run to church on Sundays. Nothing is more important than this intimate union with God. Jesus told us that the greatest commandment is this: "You shall love the Lord your God with all your heart, mind, and soul" (see Matt. 22:37; Deut. 6:5). When we prefer something over the Eucharist, we are not loving God with our entire being.

Some people say, "Why do I have to go to church? Can't I worship God where I am?" Jesus formed a community of believers. He instituted the Eucharist at the Last Supper and joined the disciples on the Road to Emmaus for the Breaking of the Bread. Church is accomplished in community, not in isolation.

Another important question we can use to examine our consciences regarding the Lord's Day is this: How do I spend the

Lord's Day? Decades ago, families would gather in their homes, have a home-cooked meal, and enjoy recreation together. Today, our Sundays might include eating out at a restaurant, going to the movie theater, shopping, or other activities. I'm as guilty as the next. But when we patronize nonessential businesses on Sundays, we are depriving others of time to worship or spend with their families. Perhaps it is time for us to reclaim Sunday for what it truly is, a day of rest, in imitation of our God, who created the world in six days and rested on the seventh.

*Mary, as you kept holy the Sabbath with your family in Nazareth, pray for me and my loved ones, that we might honor the Lord's Day in the way God intends.*

## Lenten Action

Ask yourself: "How often do I miss Mass? Why? How do I spend my Sundays?" Next Sunday, instead of going to a restaurant, make a meal at home. Instead of going shopping, play a board game with your family or read a book.

# Revering the Name of God

*"The cart drivers cannot swear without
bringing in my Son's name."*

—Our Lady of La Salette

When my mother was alive, I would often visit her and would
take her dog for a walk or take the garbage out to the dumpster
at the end of the parking lot of her apartment building. One
day, as I was undertaking one of those tasks, I heard expletive
after expletive, punctuated with name of our Lord and Savior,
Jesus Christ. I wondered, "Why was that necessary?" It was a
moment of profound sadness for me, as I heard the Lord's name
not invoked prayerfully but taken in vain.

The Second Commandment instructs us not to take the name
of the Lord in vain. How often, on a daily basis, does this happen?
In a crowd at a sporting event, Jesus' name is taken in vain. At
a bar, in casual conversation, His name is used without respect.
When I was taking in a film a while back, I was deeply disturbed
by one character's constant use of expletives sandwiched between
"Jesus" and "Christ."

"Jesus" is a sacred name, revealed by an angel to Mary as the
name given to the Savior of the world. It is the name that Jesus

said drives out demons. It is the name by which we all have been saved. It says in Sacred Scripture, "Everyone who calls on the name of the Lord will be saved" (Rom. 10:13). St. Paul says that every knee in heaven, on earth, and under the earth bends at the mention of Jesus' holy name (Phil. 2:10). It is the name of Jesus that missionaries have brought to foreign lands and proclaimed so that all might know salvation. Martyrs have died because they would not blaspheme; they would not recant their love of the sacred name of Jesus. The name of Jesus is invoked in our prayers and in our pleas for mercy. Once we realize the significance of the name of Jesus, it should sadden us when we hear it taken in vain by others and should move us to repentance for the times we also might have used Jesus' name in vain.

In (at least) two Marian apparitions, Our Lady specifically referred to the improper use of Jesus' name. In Laus, France, in an apparition that occurred in the late 1600s, Mary instructed Benoîte Rencurel to tell a nearby woman "not to curse with the name of Jesus, because if she keeps it up, there will be no paradise for her. Her conscience is in a very bad state; she should do penance." The woman, filled with tears, did reparation and corrected the course of her life. Our Lady emphasizes the consequences of such speech: "there will be no paradise" for those who take the Lord's name in vain. It makes sense. In Heaven, we will give praise to God the Father, God the Son, and God the Holy Spirit. If we do not bless God's name on earth, why would we want to do so in the Kingdom of Heaven? During this Lenten pilgrimage, let us heed Our Lady's reminder to revere the sacred name.

*Mary, teacher and model of prayer, help me always to pray as you did in your Magnificat: "Holy is His name." As you repeated the name of Jesus so often in your life as an act of love and adoration, pray for me that I may always use His name with as much reverence as you did.*

## Lenten Action

Let your ears be attentive to your surroundings. Listen for the name of Jesus spoken in public places. When you hear it, ask, "Was it a prayer? Did the speaker take God's name in vain?" If you hear the Lord's name taken in vain, say a quick prayer of reparation, such as "Jesus, I love Your holy name," "Jesus, have mercy on us sinners," "Hallowed be Thy name," or "Holy is Your name." You might wish to make it a daily practice before bed to say an Our Father with the intention of making reparation for blasphemies against the name of Jesus.

Thursday of the First Week of Lent

# Always Be Good

*"Always be good."*

—Our Lady of Beauraing

Mary spoke simple messages to the children in Beauraing, Belgium. One of her simple exhortations was "Be good." Seems easy enough, right? Sounds like something our mothers might have said when we were on our way out for the evening: "Be good tonight." Mary is asking her children to be good all the time. What might she mean?

We already examined two of the Ten Commandments, but the more difficult part is living those commandments—particularly as Jesus summarized them in the Gospels: "You shall love the Lord, your God, with all your heart, with all your soul, and with all your mind.... You shall love your neighbor as yourself" (Matt. 22:37–38). We can think of Jesus' teaching about the Good Samaritan and the command to "go and do likewise" (see Luke 10:29–37). St. Paul exhorts us always to say what good people need to hear. All of this is contained within Our Lady's request to be good.

We should examine our consciences daily and ask ourselves, "How was I not good today?" This isn't to guilt us and make us feel bad; rather, it is an opportunity to choose to live better tomorrow. If I became angry and yelled today, I can show love and be tranquil tomorrow. If I spoke badly about another person today, I can renew my commitment to say only good things tomorrow. If I drank too much today, I can live more soberly tomorrow. If I neglected my prayer today, I can pray better tomorrow.

It is hard to be good. It is easy to do evil. Today might be a good day to take a step back and look at your life and ask, "How can I be a better person?" Use your answers to create an action plan. That way, you will always strive to be good.

*Dear Blessed Mother, I want to be a good child of yours. Pray for me that I may always remain faithful to the commandments of God.*

## Lenten Action

Identify one way you can strive to be good today. Don't just think about it; act on it.

Friday of the First Week of Lent

# What Do You Need to Repent Of?

*"Are you willing to offer yourselves to God and*
*bear all the sufferings He wills to send you, as an*
*act of reparation for the conversion of sinners?*

—Our Lady of Fatima

I try to visit Lourdes once a year to spend time in prayer with Jesus and Mary. During my weeklong visits, I concelebrate the English Mass. The Mass tends to be for "orphan" pilgrims, because most pilgrims come with a group and a priest. I always enjoy speaking with people after Mass, outside the chapel, learning who they are, where they are from, and what they are praying for. One couple that caught my eye were quite young, in their early twenties. The opportunity to speak with them never presented itself; they always left the chapel hurriedly after Mass. But I ruminated on the questions in my mind: Who are they? Where are they from? What are they praying for?

As I was walking the streets on my final night in Lourdes, I happened upon the couple. I introduced myself to them and remarked on how moving it was to see them at Mass each day. It was dinnertime, so I asked them, "I'm going to get dinner. Would you like to get something to eat together?" They said yes, and we set off to find a restaurant that none of us had tried.

After we sat down at the table, I asked a question that I shouldn't have: "What do you do for a living?" The young man prefaced the question quite strangely: "Father, I can't lie to you. You are a priest after all." I wasn't prepared for the words that followed next. "I'm a thief." I immediately said, "You are joking, right?" He wasn't. "I'm a thief. I break into cars, steal things, and then sell them." Things became a little awkward. We placed our order, and I continued to press him.

Many people, when they visit the site of a Marian apparition, make it a point to go to Confession. For some people, celebrating the sacrament in this place facilitates strong conversions in their lives. I asked the young man, "Did you go to Confession while you were here?" He had. I asked him, "Did you tell the priest that you steal things?" He had. I then asked, "What was your penance?" He was told to offer his next Communion for his family.

I then decided to impart some fatherly advice to the man. "You have to stop stealing things. Your wife is here. You have a child back in England. You are going to get caught and go to jail, and what is going to happen to them? You need to find a good job." He told me that stealing was all he knew, that he lived in a bad part of town, and that he would most likely continue to steal. I've thought of this young couple and their child from time to time, and I've prayed for them, hoping that God will break through in their lives.

What troubled me the most about this conversation was that the young man evidently hadn't repented of the wrong that he had done. It seemed to me there was no purpose of amendment in his life. When we go to Confession, it seems as if we always confess the same sins, but I hope the difference between the thief and us is that we try our best not to commit these sins in the future.

The thief taught me that I needed to be repentant for my own sins. But what does repentance look like? First, we need to acknowledge something as wrong and name it. If we don't name it, we can't repent of it. Second, confessing that wrong is important. We can confess in our daily prayer, perhaps each evening before bed, during our examination of conscience. Is there anything I said or did today that I need to repent of? If there is, I can confess it in my prayer and ask God for help to do better the next day. The other way of confessing is sacramentally bringing our sins to Jesus in the confessional and receiving His pardon and absolution. Repentance involves a purpose of amendment, some concrete action that can be done to make up for what we have done. Lastly, there should be a resolution not to commit those sins in the future.

What might repentance look like for the thief with whom I had dinner? He'd have to realize that stealing is wrong and that he shouldn't take things that people have bought for themselves. Second, being sincere in prayer and confessing it would be the next step (even though he already has done the latter). Third, he probably should give some money to charity, as a way to say, "What I have doesn't belong to me — it belongs to someone else — and I'll help someone else with the money that is not rightfully mine." Lastly, his resolution to avoid stealing might include learning a trade or applying for a job so that he may no longer live that lifestyle.

What sins are present in your life? How can you repent of them?

# A Lenten Journey with Mother Mary

*Dear Blessed Mary, please pray for me, that I might have true sorrow and contrition for my sins and repent of them.*

## Lenten Action

Spend a few moments in prayer today, considering the sins you typically confess. How have you repented of them in the past? How will you repent in the future?

Saturday of the First Week of Lent

# Confess Your Sins

*"Make a general confession."*

—Our Lady of Good Help

The messages of Mary's apparitions often focus on conversion and praying for sinners. What are the first steps for the sinners for whom we pray or for our own conversion? The first steps are to acknowledge our sins and to go to Confession. That's why Our Lady requests our celebration of the sacrament of Reconciliation so often in her apparitions as well, because that is how sinners are reconciled, are forgiven, find peace, and receive sacramental grace. When Our Lady requested the Five First Saturdays devotion, one of the directions was to make a sacramental confession each month. Our Lady instructed Adele Brise, in preparation for her missionary work, to make a general confession.

When was the last time you celebrated the sacrament of Reconciliation? Some people receive the sacrament regularly, such as once a month. Others need to frequent the sacrament more often because they are conscious of grave sin. Most Catholics try to go during Advent or Lent (or both) as a way to prepare for Christmas or Easter. And then there are some who haven't received the sacrament for years or even decades, maybe even since their first confession.

As we have heard Our Lady's invitation to conversion and have examined a few key aspects of our relationship with God this week, it might be a good opportunity to celebrate the sacrament soon. The first step is to find out when the sacrament is available. Many parishes offer Confession on Saturdays. The next step is to examine your conscience. There are many good Examinations of Conscience available online that will help you become aware of the areas where you need conversion and the sins for which you have to ask for forgiveness. The last step is not chickening out but getting in your car and driving to the church. Sins can be embarrassing. You might be afraid to tell them to a priest. You might begin to talk yourself out of going, but stay strong and hold to your resolution to make a confession. Once you hear the words of absolution, you will have a strong sense of peace from knowing that you are forgiven.

*Dear Blessed Mother, you wish me to celebrate the sacrament of Reconciliation. Obtain from your Son the grace that I might have full knowledge of and contrition for my sins.*

### Lenten Action

Decide when and where you will celebrate the sacrament of Reconciliation during this Lent, and then begin to prepare by examining your conscience.

Second Week of Lent

# Praying for Others

---

Many people, when they go on pilgrimage, will bring intentions from their families and friends. When Anna went on pilgrimage, she had petitions for herself, but she also carried in her heart those she loved and their needs. This week on our Lenten pilgrimage, we will respond to Our Lady's request to pray for specific intentions as we listen to her voice and her message.

# How Do You Approach Prayer?

*"God will answer your prayers soon."*

—Our Lady of Pontmain

For years, I struggled to understand intercessory prayer. The reasons were many. Some were intellectual. For example, if God is omniscient (all-knowing), why do I need to tell Him what He already knows? Scripture tells us that God knows the number of hairs on our heads or when we sit or stand (see Matt. 10:30; Ps. 139:2). He knows the inner depths of our hearts and souls. The Gospels tell us that Jesus knew what certain people were thinking even though they didn't vocalize it (see Matt. 9:4; Luke 5:22; 11:17). If God knows all these things already, then why do I need to tell Him? Another intellectual quandary I faced related to God's immutability, His unchangeableness. God does not change. So why bother praying for others if my prayers don't persuade God? Other difficulties I faced were more personal. Lots of people asked me to pray for them or for someone they knew, but I wasn't convinced that they prayed for those people themselves. A final reason was that praying for others became overwhelming. E-mail groups I belonged to and social media accounts I followed asked for lots of prayers. The amount of prayer requests overwhelmed me so much that I didn't know if I could pray for them all, and if not, then again, why bother praying at all?

I hope you didn't stop reading after that last paragraph; otherwise you'll think I'm a priest who doesn't pray! With time, I overcame my difficulties. As I prepared my homily one Sunday for the Gospel story of Bartimaeus (Mark 10:46–52), the blind man on the side of the road, I understood why God wants us to pray. Jesus, who knows all things, asks Bartimaeus, "What do you want me to do for you?" Jesus knows he is blind. He knows that Bartimaeus wants to see. Yet He still asks. Jesus wants us to make petitionary prayers. He wants us to ask. He wants us to know that we depend on God for all that we have.

St. Augustine's letter to Proba, which is read annually in the Liturgy of the Hour's Office of Readings, helped me to realize that petitionary prayer opens our minds and hearts to God's will. Although prayer doesn't change God, it certainly does change us. As a priest, I realized that God asks me to pray for people, to offer prayers of intercession for them. All of these realizations helped me to see the value in praying for others.

What is your relationship with prayer? Do you pray only when you need something or are in a dire situation? Do you pray daily? When you pray, do you believe that God hears your prayers and answers?

In the village of Pontmain, Our Lady appeared in a blue dress, adorned with a crown, and holding a crucifix. She remained in the sky, visible only to the children, not even to the people gathered nearby. Words began to appear in the sky, bearing Mary's message for the people. She told them, "But do pray, my children; God will answer your prayers soon." During this Lenten season, when you don't want to pray for someone, remember Our Lady's encouragement to pray, and if you doubt that God answers prayers, recall her words: "God will answer your prayers soon."

*Dear Blessed Mother, you are always interceding for your children here below. Help me to pray as you do for those who are in need.*

## Lenten Action

Make a list of people you want to pray for this week. Each day, say a prayer for them, either a prayer of your own words or a Hail Mary or some other prayer.

Monday of the Second Week of Lent

# Do You Avoid Prayer?

*"Where are you going? Where are you headed?"*

—Our Lady of Guadalupe

The Blessed Mother interrupted the life of Juan Diego when she appeared to him. He had just gone to Mass and was on his way to care for his uncle Bernadino, who was sick. Our Lady asked Juan to bring a message to the bishop. Juan did what was asked of him but received no satisfaction from His Excellency. Anxious to tend to his uncle and thus wishing to avoid the Lady and the delay she might cause, he took another route. But no one can run from Our Lady. She found Juan and asked him, "Where are you headed?" It was as if she was saying, "Why are you avoiding me?"

Could Our Lady say the same thing to us? Could Jesus ask us the same question? During our Lenten journey, we are striving to be more faithful to and regular in prayer. Before Lent began, what was your prayer life like? How did you pray? How often? Everyone's experience of prayer is different. Some people pray only when they are in a pinch and need divine help. Others have minimal prayer in their life: praying only memorized prayers in the morning, before meals, or before bed. The prayer life of other people is rather mechanical — like a to-do list; they know what they want to do, and they do it as soon as they can or as quickly as they can, so they can check it off their list. As we continue through this Lenten devotional, we will have many opportunities for different types of prayer. In the second week and continuing into the third week of Lent, we will focus on specific prayer petitions each day. During the fourth week of Lent, we will try different methods of prayer that Our Lady taught and requested when she appeared. I hope you will find a few methods of prayer that work for you.

Back to the question at hand: What has your relationship with prayer been like?

If our relationship with prayer could be better, it is good for us to examine the reasons why we haven't prayed as much as we should. It's a question related to why we avoid prayer. A common answer comes down to time. "I don't have enough time to pray." We are all busy. Lots of tasks and responsibilities demand our time. The most important time for prayer each week is at Sunday Mass, but to have a strong relationship with God, we need to talk to Him daily. Could you pray during your commute to work? While going for a short walk? If you drive by a church every day and it is open, could you make a quick visit to the Blessed Sacrament? I heard it said that God knows our screen-time reports and how long we watched Netflix or Hulu in a given week. When we go before the Lord, if we haven't given Him due time in prayer, He might tell us that some of that time could have been used for prayer.

Another reason we might avoid prayer is that we are afraid of what God might ask of us. If I deepen my friendship with Jesus, He might ask me to do something I don't want to do. As I pray over His Word in Scripture, I might be challenged to forgive someone I want to hold a grudge against, or He might give new direction to my life. Praying to God might intimidate you. If it does, ask the Lord to calm those fears and give you His peace.

Doubt can stand in the way of prayer. We might erroneously believe that God does not care about us or listen to us, so we avoid prayer, thinking it to be a waste of time.

We might also avoid prayer because we don't know how or where to pray. During the next several weeks, I hope you will learn a few ways to pray and will be taught the language of prayer, but the "where" you will need to decide for yourself.

These are just a few reasons why we might not pray as much as we should. I'm sure there are more. Spend time evaluating your prayer life so that you can identify what it is that keeps you from praying.

*Mary, you made yourself available to God by praying, "Let it be done to me according to your will." Pray for me each day, that I might find time to pray and deepen my friendship with Jesus.*

## Lenten Action

Pause for a few minutes right now and think about your prayer life for the past few weeks. Why have you prayed? Why have you neglected prayer? What is your hope for prayer in the weeks ahead, but most importantly, after Divine Mercy Sunday (the Sunday after Easter)?

# Whose Conversion Are You Praying For?

*"Offer your Communion for the conversion of sinners."*

—Our Lady of Good Help

I've been on social media for more than twelve years. I started my personal account right after I graduated from high school and before I started college. I have a public page in addition to managing pages for parishes and other organization to which I belong. I receive a number of personal friend requests each week—some from people of the past, others from people whom I have some familiarity with, and others from people who have read my writings online. I accept the requests of people I know and hesitate to do so with those I don't know.

After being on Facebook for over a decade, I have friends from high school, from the college I attended, from the college seminary I transferred to, from the major seminary I graduated from, and from my parish assignments. I formed some close friendships with people I went to school with, but as the years go by, we grow distant; it's difficult to stay in touch with some people. One friend began to live a life contrary to the Catholic Faith and became a vocal opponent of the Church. When I would scroll through my newsfeed, I would often see his posts. When I brought it up to another friend, he told me, "I unfriended him months ago." I wondered why I had not yet done that. One day, as I was praying in the church, the reason hit me: I had not unfriended him because he needed someone to pray for him. His posts became an invitation to pray, especially for his conversion.

When Mary appeared to Adele Brise, she told her that, as the Queen of Heaven, she prays for the conversion of sinners, and she also said, "I wish for you to do the same. Offer your Holy Communion for that intention." We all know people who need the grace of conversion. Maybe some of our family members no longer go to church or are not even baptized. We might have a friend who struggles with alcoholism. We don't judge these people, but when we see how they live their lives, hear what they say, or notice troubling patterns, those are occasions for prayer.

Whoever it is, whatever it is, you might feel unable to help them, but know that you are not, because you have prayer on your side. Begin to pray daily for these loved ones, and see what God will do in their lives.

*Dear Blessed Mother, you know my family and friends. Ask your Son to help them in whatever areas they struggle and flood their lives with God's grace.*

## Lenten Action

Spend a few moments today thinking about the people you know. Is there one in particular whom you think of right away? Adopt that person in prayer this Lenten season. As you make an act of self-denial, pray: "O Jesus, I do this act out of love for You and for the conversion of N.'s soul."

Wednesday of the Second Week of Lent

# For Respect for Life

*"My youngest and dearest son, these different kinds of flowers
are the proof, the sign that you will take to the bishop."*

—Our Lady of Guadalupe

Our Lady asked St. Juan Diego to take the roses he found and
show them to the bishop. He gathered them in his cloak and
took them to His Excellency. When presenting the roses, Juan
and the bishop discovered the miraculous image imprinted on
Juan's tilma. The image contains much symbolism and reads like
an icon. One important aspect of the image depicts Our Lady
wearing a pregnancy belt, common in the Aztec culture. Cultur-
ally significant, Mary appears as a pregnant woman, who will give
birth to God incarnate, in a culture in which people often offered
their infants as sacrifices to pagan gods. Mary's message to Juan
Diego draws the Aztec people to worship the true, living God.

Mary loves life. Just as she grieved over the infants being
offered to false gods, Mary certainly must have been sad when
Herod ordered the execution of all male infants in hopes that he
would kill Jesus. Mary weeps over the travesty of abortion today
because all life is sacred. The image of Our Lady of Guadalupe
has become an icon for the pro-life movement.

# A Lenten Journey with Mother Mary

Marian devotion is part of many aspects of pro-life prayer vigils. Many participants pray the Rosary outside abortion clinics in hopes of obtaining conversion of heart for the woman contemplating abortion and for those who work in the clinics. The Joyful Mysteries of the Rosary emphasize the sacredness of life, leading us to contemplate Jesus' conception, the meeting of John and Jesus in the womb, and the birth of Jesus. Praying the Rosary helps us to reflect on the beauty and gift of human life. Paintings and statues of Mary sometimes show her pregnant. All of these are reminders of how Mary wants us to pray for respect for life. Today let us pray for those contemplating abortion, for the healing of those who have had abortions, and for the conversion of those who work in the abortion industry.

*Our Lady of Guadalupe, patroness of the unborn, obtain from your Son the grace of conversion for those who do not value the gift of human life.*

## Lenten Action

Coinciding with Lent, 40 Days for Life hosts around-the-clock prayer vigils in many cities throughout the world. Have you ever been a part of a peaceful prayer vigil? Try to make time this Lent to pray in front of an abortion clinic. If you are unable to do so, practice your Lenten almsgiving by donating to a local pregnancy resource center.

Thursday of the Second Week of Lent

# For Peace in the World

*"Say the Rosary every day, to bring peace to*
*the world and the end of the war."*

—Our Lady of Fatima

Many of Mary's messages concern peace. This was the case in Fatima, where she requested the praying of the Rosary every day for peace in the world and to facilitate the end of World War I. Peace was the concern of her motherly heart in Rwanda, knowing that if hearts didn't change, the Rwandan genocide would occur. It is evident from her messages that Mary does not like war, death, devastation, and the tearing apart of families. What she does love is peace, when countries put aside differences and work for the common good. It is said that Our Lady of Fatima was essential in bringing about the end of the Cold War.

Since Our Lady's apparitions in Fatima in 1917, another world war occurred, and other wars happened in the late 1900s. And then there are the wars that we might not even know about between small countries.

Why did Our Lady recommend praying the Rosary for peace in the world? There could be any number of reasons. Perhaps, when we pray the Rosary, Our Lady teaches us about her Son, who willed peace for the world. Or maybe, through the continuous invocation "pray for us sinners," Mary indeed does that, praying for those who wish to choose war and violence.

Today the world continues to be entrenched in war and conflict. There are senseless attacks almost daily, causing the deaths of so many. The threat of terrorism looms, forcing people to live in fear. If Our Lady appeared today (some allege that she does), part of her message would likely be to pray for peace. She would ask us to pray for the conversion of government leaders, that they will not take lives but strive always to preserve peace. Today we respond to Our Lady's request to pray for peace in the world, and as we do so, we will become the peacemakers our world desperately needs.

*Queen of Peace, obtain for our world the conversion of hearts necessary so that we might be free from war and terrorism.*

## Lenten Action

Pray the Rosary today. Before you begin, state your intention: for peace in the world.

Friday of the Second Week of Lent

# Name Your Grace

*"The ball which you see represents the whole world, especially France, and each person in particular. These rays symbolize the graces I shed upon those who ask for them. The gems from which rays do not fall are the graces for which souls forget to ask."*

—Our Lady of the Miraculous Medal

When it comes to prayer, it is important to know for what we are praying. We need to be intentional in our asking. When I was a newly ordained priest, it all seemed surreal to me. Am I really a priest? Do I really confect the Eucharist? One morning before the Blessed Sacrament, these questions flooded my heart. I decided to turn them over to the Lord. And one way that I did that was by being bold in my prayer. I said to God, "Show me that my priesthood is real." God came through that very day through a powerful pastoral experience in which I happened to be in the right place at the right time. On another day, I was scheduled to hear confessions at one of my parishes. There had been a drought in terms of people receiving the sacrament. As I celebrated my morning Mass, I petitioned God to send someone to the confessional. Later that evening, someone did come to Confession. God answered my prayer.

I offer similar counsel in the confessional about sin. If a person struggles with impatience, I tell him to pray for patience; if someone is angry, to pray for charity; if impure, to pray for purity. Today you are invited to name your grace. Ask God to do something in your life. Pray to grow in a certain virtue. Name your grace. Pray for it daily, and see what God does for you!

*Dear Lord, hear the prayers that I offer You each day, and bestow Your manifold graces upon me.*

## Lenten Action

At the beginning of each day, formulate an intention for the day, asking for God's help. At the end of the day, look back and see what God provided at your request.

Saturday of the Second Week of Lent

# For an Increase in Marian Devotion

*"Am I not here, I who am your Mother? Are you not*
*under my shadow and protection? Am I not the source of*
*your joy? Are you not in the hollow of my mantle, in the*
*crossing of my arms? Do you need something more?"*

—Our Lady of Guadalupe

Out of all the Christian denominations, the Catholic Church
has the most prominent devotion to Mary, the Mother of Jesus.
Not just Roman Catholics but also Eastern Catholics have a
beautiful devotion as well in the many homilies of saints and in
their hymns. Some Protestant denominations, such as Anglicans,
have a semblance of Marian piety. And other Protestants are
beginning to look to Mary as an example of lived Christianity,
especially in regard to being a disciple of Jesus.

Even Catholics who are devoted to Mary are not as many as
one might hope or want. There was a period in the Church in the
twentieth century when Marian devotion was frowned upon in
favor of a more liturgical-centered spirituality. With the papacies
of Pope John Paul II and Pope Francis, Marian devotion has been
on the rise. Apparitions of Our Lady also help to facilitate a deeper
love for Mary's role in the salvation of the world. A pilgrim who

visits a Marian shrine might not have a strong devotion or have none at all. But that pilgrim might leave with a greater love for Mary and a rosary in hand from the gift store.

We are saddened when we think of those who do not love Mary or see her as their mother and intercessor. The Five First Saturdays associated with the Fatima apparitions are to be offered in reparation for blasphemies against the Immaculate Conception, her virginity, her divine maternity and her motherhood of all people, indifference and hatred toward her, and insults toward sacred images of her. It might seem as if Our Lady addresses those who discount the privileges given to her by God. When I first read about these reasons, I immediately thought about Protestants who do not understand Mary. Our Marian devotion must not be excessive but should be attractive to those who might not understand it.

Our Lady reminded Juan Diego that she was his mother. Today we remember that Mary is our mother and protects us by her intercession. She brings us joy because she brought to the world our salvation. As we bask in Mary's motherhood of all believers, let us entrust to Mary all believers, those who acknowledge her as mother and those who do not, so that one day they may know her as the source of their joy.

*Dear Blessed Mother, I know you are my mother. Remind me of this frequently. I entrust to your intercession all of your children, that one day all might know you as their mother.*

## Lenten Action

Every time you pass by a statue or an image of Mary in your home, look at it and say: "She's my mother." If you don't have a statue or a picture of Mary in your home, buy one!

Third Week of Lent

# Intentional Prayer Continued

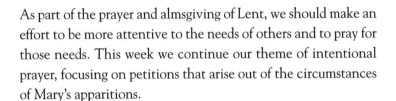

As part of the prayer and almsgiving of Lent, we should make an effort to be more attentive to the needs of others and to pray for those needs. This week we continue our theme of intentional prayer, focusing on petitions that arise out of the circumstances of Mary's apparitions.

Third Sunday of Lent

# For the Souls in Purgatory

*Lucia asked about two young women who had died recently, and Our Lady of Fatima told her that one was in heaven and the other, her friend Amelia, would be in purgatory "until the end of world."*

Whether you realize it or not, every Mass you go to has an assigned intention. More often than not, Masses are offered for the souls of the faithful departed, though Masses can be offered for the living too. To have a Mass said for a loved one who has died, you would visit the parish office to schedule the Mass and pay a stipend, usually about ten dollars. Each weekend, every parish offers a Mass intention *pro populo*, or "for the people," all the living and deceased of the parish. This Mass intention ensures that no soul is ever forgotten.

Two Marian apparitions have a powerful connection to the Holy Souls in Purgatory. The apparitions in Knock, Ireland, occurred the day after the parish priest, Archdeacon Cavanagh, completed his hundredth Mass for the Holy Souls in Purgatory. These two happenings, the completion of Masses and the apparition, seem to coincide, and this draws our attention to the efficacy of the Mass for the Holy Souls. In Fatima, when Our Lady appeared to the three children, they asked Our Lady about the souls of those who had died. About their friend Amelia, Our Lady said she would be in Purgatory for a very long time. Some versions say until the end of the world, but the critical documents of Fatima support the former, not the latter. The mention of Purgatory and the state of their friend's soul encouraged the Fatima children to pray for Amelia. We should never canonize our loved ones who have died — never assume they are already in Heaven. Instead, we should remember them in our prayers often, praying for their souls.

Author Susan Tassone, known by many as "the Purgatory Lady" because of her writings on the topic, reminds people of a teaching of St. Thomas Aquinas: that if a person for whom we pray or have Masses offered is already in Heaven, that person experiences an increase in his accidental glory — that is to say, the power of his intercession for his loved ones. There are many stories about souls who, after they died, have visited those they left behind and requested Masses to be offered. In *The Glories of Mary*, St. Alphonsus Liguori tells such a story about Sister Catherine of St. Augustine, who had the custom of praying for the dead of the village. There was one soul for whom she neglected to pray. The deceased woman asked for her prayers and for Masses to be offered so that she could soon enter Heaven. The Mass is a powerful prayer for the dead. Have Masses said for your loved ones. Visit their graves often. Never cease to pray for them.

*Dear Blessed Mother, whom we ask to pray for us at the hour of our death, by your prayers, obtain from your Son relief for the Holy Souls and lead them soon to the Kingdom of Heaven.*

*For the Souls in Purg*

Lenten Act

Write a list of all your deceas
friends. After each name, pra'
him [or her]." If it has been a
offered for your relatives, consid

71

Monday of the Third Week of Lent

# For the Dying

*"Do not let your uncle's illness pressure you*
*with grief, because he will not die of it now.*
*You may be certain that he is already well."*

—Our Lady of Guadalupe

In hospitals throughout the world, there are people dying right now. Others are dying in nursing homes or in the comfort of their homes, thanks to the care of hospice. Their families are gathered at their bedsides, and they are saying their final goodbyes.

It's hard to lose someone you love. I remember flying home to be with my grandma in her last days as she was in ICU. It was a time of sadness, because she had supported me throughout my life. It was also a time of letting go; I knew that now she would have no more pain, but only peace and joy in the Kingdom.

Juan Diego had a great concern for his uncle who was dying. He was about to or already had received the last rites (today we call this Anointing of the Sick). Hope for a healing was lost. So imagine Juan's surprise when he heard Our Lady say these words to him about his uncle, and Juan's amazement when he saw his uncle. We can envision the many healings of Jesus in Scripture and how He gave new life to those who came to Him.

# A Lenten Journey with Mother Mary

When someone dies, especially if we have prayed that the person might be healed, we might be overcome with doubt and wonder why our prayer was not answered by God. The book of Ecclesiastes reminds us that there is a time to live and a time to die. God invites us to change our perspective on death and to realize that our loved ones are still alive in eternity. They are still active in our lives, praying for us from their place in eternity. The death of a loved one should move us to give thanks for that person's life and what he meant to us.

Today we focus our intercessory prayer on the dying, that they may have comfort and peace as they go before the Lord, and also for those who love them, as they mourn and grieve.

*Dear Blessed Mother, as you were close to Juan Diego's uncle and obtained his healing, I entrust to your intercession those who are in the last moments of their lives. Obtain for them forgiveness, comfort, and peace as they leave this world and inherit the one promised by God.*

## Lenten Action

Do you know someone who is dying? Go and visit that person. Make a meal for the person's family. Bring words of comfort. Do you know someone who has experienced a loss? Send that person a text, a message, or a card to let him know you are thinking of him.

Tuesday of the Third Week of Lent

# For Bishops

*"Go to the residence of the Bishop of Mexico, and you will
tell him how I am sending you, so that you may reveal to him
that I very much want him to build me a house here, to erect a
temple for me on the plain; you will tell him everything, all that
you have seen and marveled at, and what you have heard."*

—Our Lady of Guadalupe

In many of Mary's apparitions, the bishop played an important
role. That was the case in the apparitions received by Juan
Diego at Tepeyac. Our Lady instructed Juan to tell the bishop
all that had happened and to request that a church be built
where she had appeared. Like most people, the bishop did
not believe Juan and asked for a sign. As you can imagine,
Our Lady delivered. She showed Juan where some roses were
miraculously growing, although it was winter, and told him
to gather some to take to the bishop. Juan collected the roses
in his tilma, ran to the bishop's house, and let the flowers fall
from his tilma. The bishop knelt in amazement, not because of
the flowers, but because of the miraculous image of Our Lady
imprinted on Juan's tilma. That same tilma is venerated to this
day by pilgrims to Guadalupe.

# A Lenten Journey with Mother Mary

The bishop played an important role in the Guadalupian events. This should remind us that we need to pray for our bishops. In recent years, the shameful cover-ups of sexual abuse of minors by some priests and bishops and misappropriate handling of church resources has caused scandal among the faithful, leading them to lose faith in the Church's hierarchy. Some have even walked away from the Church because of it.

It is easy for us to fixate on the minority of bishops who have failed the Church, but more importantly, there are heroic bishops who faithfully served the Church, and their lives give witness to that. St. Oscar Romero comes to mind as one who heroically saved his people and stood strong in the face of opposition. Many were inspired by the example of Archbishop Fulton Sheen. And there are countless other bishops who have tirelessly served God to the best of their ability with little recognition or notice. During this penitential season of Lent, amid scandal, let us offer our prayers for the bishops of the Church, and maybe even offer small sacrifices in reparation for their sins.

*Dear Mary, you are the Mother of the Church. Be a mother to your bishops, and entrust the entire college of bishops throughout the world to your Son's merciful love.*

## Lenten Action

Say a prayer for your local bishop. Ask God to inspire him in the way he governs, teaches, preaches, and sanctifies.

# For Priests

*"You will tell the priests to have a chapel built here."*

—Our Lady of Lourdes

Clergy play an important role in Mary's apparitions. The visionaries come under their pastoral care. Often, Our Lady requested that the seers speak with the local pastors. In yesterday's meditation, we saw that Mary asked Juan Diego to make a request of the local bishop. In Lourdes, Our Lady instructed St. Bernadette to ask the pastor for a chapel to be built. Bernadette did this, and the priest told her to ask the woman her name. When Bernadette reported that Our Lady said she was the Immaculate Conception, the pastor went from being a skeptic to being a believer, because there was no way an illiterate, uneducated peasant girl would know of this belief about Our Lady, which had been defined as a dogma only a few years before.

In Champion, Wisconsin, Our Lady did not tell Adele to speak to the priest, but Adele knew she needed counsel after seeing the mysterious vanishing woman twice. The priest instructed her to ask the woman, "In God's name, who are you, and what do you want of me?" This initial question prompted Adele's heavenly visitor to speak, identifying herself as the Queen of Heaven, but also directing Adele to the sacraments—to the Eucharist and Confession. By highlighting the sacramental life of the Church, Our Lady emphasized the priesthood, because without the priest, there is no Eucharist; without the priest, there is no absolution.

The role of the clergy in conveying Our Lady's message to the world invites us to pray for priests: in reparation for past sins, for the conversion of unfaithful priests, for the sanctification of all the clergy, and in thanksgiving for priests in our lives. For every unfaithful priest who has brought scandal upon the priesthood, there are countless faithful priests who spend their lives dedicated to God, in service to the Church and the faithful. Although there are concrete actions that can be done to reform the clergy, we must not forget the spiritual—offering our prayers and sacrifices for those who offer the Holy Sacrifice of the Mass.

In my own priesthood, the prayers of the faithful have sustained me in difficult moments. Your prayers today for the clergy might be exactly what they need right now.

*Dear Jesus, just as You called the first apostles to be Your priests, You continue to call forth men for service in the Church. Forgive those who offended the sacred duty of their office, and bestow healing upon Your Church. Sanctify the priests of Your Church, especially those I know. Draw them into Your Eucharistic Presence; convert their hearts; reveal Your goodness to them. Thank You for all who have faithfully served Your Church and who have ministered to me throughout my life.*

## Lenten Action

Make a list of all the priests who have blessed your life: the priest who baptized you, the priest who heard your last Confession, the pastor of your parish, and any other priest who has impacted you. Pray for them, and consider writing some of them notes of encouragement.

Thursday of the Third Week of Lent

# For the Grace to Say Yes

*"Listen, my youngest and dearest son, know for sure
that I have no lack of servants, of messengers, to whom I
can give the task of carrying my breath, my word, so that
they carry out my will. But it is very necessary that you,
personally, go and plead that my wish, my will, become
a reality, be carried out through your intercession."*

—Our Lady of Guadalupe

Juan Diego was very reticent about Our Lady's request of him. He
considered himself unworthy of the task before him. He thought
Our Lady could have asked someone better. He wanted to say
no. Eventually he said yes. The same was true for Adele Brise.
She asked: "What more can I do, for I know so little myself?" She
did not think she was capable of teaching the children because
her education was meager. Yet God used her, and she taught the
children their Faith.

In our own lives, we often want to say no when someone
asks us to do something. We do need to discern the requests
that come our way. We might want to examine the reasons we
want to say no. Are they good reasons? Or are our responses
motivated by fear?

# A Lenten Journey with Mother Mary

One of the greatest examples of a person who said yes is our Blessed Mother. Something unexpected happened in the life of Mary when she was a young woman. An angel appeared to her and told her that she was going to be a mother. After hearing everything, Mary said, "Let it be done to me according to your word." She said yes to being Jesus' Mother, and that yes changed the world, because Mary gave birth to the Savior and Redeemer of the world.

*Inspired by your example, O Mary, I pray that I will at all times strive to do God's will in my life by saying yes.*

## Lenten Action

The next time someone asks you to do something, no matter how small, say yes, and don't complain.

Friday of the Third Week of Lent

# For Interior Peace

*"Go and fear nothing. I will help you."*

— Our Lady in Champion, Wisconsin

*"Let nothing else worry you, disturb you."*

—Our Lady of Guadalupe

At the Annunciation, Mary received a visit from the angel Gabriel, who told her she would be the Mother of the Savior. After greeting Mary, the first words of Gabriel were "Do not be afraid." Receiving a heavenly visitor who speaks a message about your future might be a frightening experience. The angel wanted to put Mary at peace by saying those words. Isn't it interesting that in some of Mary's messages, she echoes those words? "Go and fear nothing." "Let nothing else worry you." Mary wants us to have interior peace.

So many things worry us. We allow them to take away our inner peace. A few years ago, I wondered where God would lead me as a priest. I had my own aspirations, dreams, and goals. One day, it seemed as if they would come to fruition, and the next day, it seemed very unlikely. I happened to be visiting a Schoenstatt convent of sisters in the Milwaukee area during that time.

# A Lenten Journey with Mother Mary

Although I had a plan for how I would spend my afternoon and had a very strict timeline, the sister whom I was visiting told me I might want to visit their shrine chapel while I was there.

I could easily have ignored the sister's request, because to do so would mean that I would not do what I thought I wanted to do later in the day. As I deliberated, my conscience got the best of me, and I prayed for an hour in the chapel. During that prayer, I offered to Mary my worries about the future. And in that prayer, I sensed Mary telling me, "Don't worry, I have a plan for you." It was a powerful experience for me. Ever since, whenever struggles arise in my life, I remember that experience and those consoling words. And wouldn't you know, some of those aspirations and dreams have been realized since. There truly was a plan.

What is taking away your interior peace? Maybe Mary's words to Adele, to Juan, and even to me are meant for you today.

*Dear Blessed Mother, help me to hear the words you heard and to live the words you speak. Intercede for me so that all fear and useless anxiety may be put to rest in my mind and heart.*

### Lenten Action

When you find yourself worried today, repeat the words "Do not be afraid." Hopefully, as you do, you will be strengthened to face whatever the day brings.

Saturday of the Third Week of Lent

# For Pilgrims

*"Why do you come here?" asked one
of the visionaries. Mary answered:
"So people come here on pilgrimage."*

—Our Lady of Beauraing

We are all pilgrims. This book is, in some sense, a spiritual pilgrimage through Lent, listening to the voice of our heavenly mother. We are pilgrims during our earthly exile to the heavenly Jerusalem. It should not be surprising that the places where Mary appeared have become heavily visited places of prayer. Claims of the supernatural always attract people, believers and unbelievers alike.

Pilgrims include those who have a strong connection to their Faith and regularly practice it. Other pilgrims visit a place out of urgency. If a Marian shrine is near one's residence, one may visit frequently and entrust his petitions to the intercession of Our Lady. Or he might stop and light a candle for someone who is sick. Other people who have an urgent intention might travel hundreds or thousands of miles to pray at a holy site. Still other pilgrims might be merely curious or even unaware. Maybe they have heard people talk about the site, and they want to check it out for themselves, or perhaps they haven't heard about it, but friends take them there. Pilgrims come from all walks of life and backgrounds, with different reasons for their visits.

A pilgrimage can be a time of conversion and grace. Some people might visit a shrine as skeptics, unbelievers, or hardened sinners, only to have their hearts conquered by the gospel of Jesus Christ. When I have heard confessions in Lourdes as an auxiliary confessor, I've often thought that people are drawn to the site because of Our Lady, and once they spend a few minutes at the grotto, they feel called to go to Confession.

As we make our spiritual pilgrimage through the Lenten season to the various apparition sites of Our Lady and listen to her message, there are at the same time hundreds upon hundreds, thousands upon thousands, who are visiting these shrines right now. Although we are not there physically, we can pray for those who are. We can pray with them for whatever their intentions are by asking that God's will be done. We can pray that God will make His presence known in the lives of those who may have doubts. We can pray that those who visit these holy places will experience a profound conversion of life and commitment to the Faith.

*Lord, You hear the cry of the poor. Hear the prayers of Your people who visit the places where Mary has appeared. Through the intercession of Our Lady, bestow many graces upon them and their families. Give them the grace of conversion and fidelity.*

## Lenten Action

Plan to become a Marian pilgrim. If you are able, visit a local Marian shrine, or make a visit to an altar statue of Mary. If you can't make a physical pilgrimage, consider a spiritual pilgrimage using Marge Fenelon's *Mary, My Queen and Mother: A Living Novena.*

Fourth Week of Lent

# Mary Teaches Us Methods of Prayer

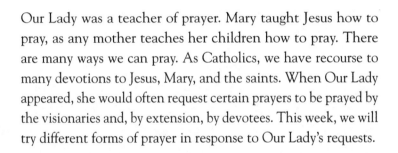

Our Lady was a teacher of prayer. Mary taught Jesus how to pray, as any mother teaches her children how to pray. There are many ways we can pray. As Catholics, we have recourse to many devotions to Jesus, Mary, and the saints. When Our Lady appeared, she would often request certain prayers to be prayed by the visionaries and, by extension, by devotees. This week, we will try different forms of prayer in response to Our Lady's requests.

Fourth Sunday of Lent

# Morning and Evening Prayer

*"Do you say your prayers well, my children?" she asked the*
*shepherds. Both answered with complete frankness: "Not*
*very well, Madam." "Ah, my children," she exhorted them,*
*"you must be sure to say them well morning and evening.*
*When you cannot do better, say at least an Our Father*
*and a Hail Mary; but when you have time, say more."*

—Our Lady of La Salette

Our Lady always asks her seers to pray. Sometimes it is just the encouragement to pray, and other times it is a very direct request: "This is how you should pray." During this week, we will identify different prayers Our Lady requested and put them into practice in our daily lives. Sometimes people feel burdened by all the requests for different prayers through private revelations. It can be overwhelming to think about praying the Rosary every day, and the Divine Mercy Chaplet, and being devoted to the Sacred Heart, and the Precious Blood, and so forth. I often wonder whether, if we prayed all the prayers requested through private revelation, there would be enough time in the day to eat and sleep! What I do make out of all of it is that God is trying to teach us to pray and wants us to pray more frequently. Although it is noble for a person to want to do everything Our Lady has requested, it might be best to pray a few devotions well than simply to repeat words and "babble like the pagans" (Matt. 6:7).

When I read the message of La Salette, the simplicity of the request for prayer struck me. Our Lady asked the children to be sure they prayed every day, even if it was simply at night and was an Our Father and a Hail Mary. This is often the way parents begin teaching their children how to pray. Perhaps the lesson of La Salette regarding prayer is to get the simple things right first, before we begin to tackle larger ambitions regarding prayer. Given that we already considered the question of whether we avoid prayer, we might evaluate how our prayer lives have been thus far during Lent. If you need to, recommit yourself to basic prayers for starters.

*Dear Blessed Mother, you were a faithful woman of prayer. Please obtain for me the grace of fidelity to prayer from your Son.*

## Lenten Action

Ask God how He wants you to pray every day. Make a prayer resolution, and at the end of each day, ask yourself, "Have I prayed in the way I wanted today?"

Monday of the Fourth Week of Lent

# The Daily Rosary

*"I want you to come here on the thirteenth of next month
[August], to continue to pray the Rosary every day in honor of
Our Lady of the Rosary, in order to obtain peace for the world
and the end of the war, because only she can help you."*

—Our Lady of Fatima

The Rosary is a beautiful prayer. St. Louis de Montfort reflected
that the Rosary affords the devotee an opportunity to pray
through the life of Christ. The repetition of the Hail Mary allows
us ample time to consider the life of Jesus. If you have difficulty
focusing on the Mysteries of the Rosary, the method I teach in
my book *A Rosary Litany* might help you.

The Rosary is an important prayer for many reasons. One is
that Mary herself asked us to pray it every day for peace in the
world when she appeared to the Fatima children. If Mary asked
for its daily recitation, it is a very important prayer, and who are
we to suggest that such a request should be ignored (granted, we
need not believe in Marian apparitions)? In a different apparition, Our Lady entrusted fifteen promises of the Rosary to Blessed
Alan de la Roche. Again, an overview of those promises might
compel us to pray the Rosary with greater frequency.

# A Lenten Journey with Mother Mary

The Rosary provides a means to obtain grace. Mary presents our prayers before God's throne when we ask her to pray for us. Events such as the Christians' victory over the Turks at Lepanto suggest that praying the Rosary collectively is efficacious. St. Louis de Montfort also taught that when you pray the Rosary as an individual, you gain graces for one Rosary, but when you pray it with a hundred people, you gain the graces of a hundred Rosaries. The graces we receive are not only answers to the intentions we offer during the Rosary, but the graces that God wishes to give us because of our devotion.

The concluding petition of the Hail Mary—"pray for us sinners now and at the hour of our death"—is also very powerful. Praying the Rosary every day and saying those words so many times gives us a greater assurance that Mary will hold true to our most often asked request. The concluding prayer often recited at the end of the Rosary asks that we may imitate what the mysteries contain and obtain what they promise. We wish to imitate the virtues connected to each mystery and the promise that they give us as believers.

What is your relationship with the Rosary? Are you a daily devotee? Irregular? Do you wish you prayed it more? Maybe this is the Lent to make a conscious effort to pray the Rosary with greater frequency. When considering incorporating the Rosary into your life, identify when a good time each day would be to pray it. I love praying the Rosary while I walk or drive. But I also enjoy doing so in the church and with others. Find what works for you, and once you pray it more often, I'm certain you will notice that God is doing great things in your life.

*Mary, I know you want me to pray the Rosary every day.*
*Give me the desire and the motivation to do so.*

## Lenten Action

Today, pray five decades of the Rosary. Notice what you like about it and what your struggles are. If you continue praying the Rosary, you might wish to pray with an app or use a meditation book.

# The Seven Sorrows of Mary

*"What I am asking you to do is repent. If you say the Rosary of the Seven Sorrows and meditate on it well, you will find all the strength you need to repent of your sins and convert your heart."*

—Our Lady of Kibeho

Among the many devotions to Mary, one similar to the Dominican Rosary (that is, the more traditional Rosary of Joyful, Luminous, Sorrowful, and Glorious Mysteries) is the Seven Sorrows of Mary Rosary, in which one reflects on the sorrowful moments of Mary's life as a mother. The devotion finds its origin in Scripture, because Mary's heart would be pierced by a sword of sorrow. Mary knew this early on, and many of the sorrows occurred during the last days of Jesus' life. Mary at the foot of the Cross embodies what it means to be a sorrowful mother.

The devotion became associated with the Servite Order (a religious community), who have been the promoters of the devotion since the thirteenth century. Along the way, many other saints, such as Bridget of Sweden, wrote about the Seven Sorrows, and Pope Pius VII officially approved the devotion.

After the Sign of the Cross, the Seven Sorrows Rosary begins with the recitation of the Act of Contrition as a way to call to mind our sorrow for sins. Then three Hail Marys are prayed, followed by this prayer: "Most Merciful Mother, remind us always about the Sorrows of your Son, Jesus." For each of the seven mysteries of this Rosary, one prays an Our Father, seven Hail Marys, and the "Most Merciful Mother" prayer. The mysteries are:

1. The prophecy of Simeon
2. The flight into Egypt
3. The losing of the Christ Child in the Temple
4. The meeting of Jesus and Mary on the way of the Cross
5. Mary standing at the foot of the cross
6. Mary holding Jesus' lifeless body
7. Mary witnessing the burial of Jesus

Conclude with this prayer: "Queen of Martyrs, your heart suffered so much. I beg you, by the merits of the tears you shed in these terrible and sorrowful times, to obtain for me and all the sinners of the world the grace of complete sincerity and repentance. Amen." Then pray three times, "Mary, who was conceived without sin and who suffered for us, pray for us" and make the Sign of the Cross.

Mary asked one of the Kibeho visionaries to pray the Rosary of the Seven Sorrows. Praying this Rosary helps us call to mind Mary's suffering. It allows us to walk with Mary during the Passion and console her in her grief. Jesus died for the sins of the world. Mary mourns over our sinfulness and asks us to repent. She believes that praying the Seven Sorrows Rosary will help facilitate our repentance. Our mom knows best. Let's listen to her advice and today put into action what she requests.

*Dear Blessed Mother, I wish to know your suffering. Please pray for me that I may repent of my sins and convert my heart.*

## Lenten Action

Pray the Seven Sorrows Rosary. You will need to use your fingers to count the Hail Marys for each set of mysteries. As you pray, consider how Mary mourns over our sins and wants us to experience joy and the fullness of life detached from sin.

# Silent Prayer

Mary, Joseph, John, and a lamb on an altar appeared to a group
of people outside the parish church in Knock, Ireland. Unique
to this apparition was the silence. There was no message. Mary
and the others remained with the onlookers, who looked up
in amazement and wonder. They saw something not all people
are privileged to see. They saw the glories of Heaven while on
earth. And all they could do was to be silent, just as Mary and
the rest were.

Are you afraid of silence? Many people are! When we drive,
we do so with the radio on or Pandora playing. When we do
things around the house or go for a walk, we have to listen
to something. The television is often on as background noise,
whether a person listens or not. In the idle moments of our lives,
we open our phones and scroll through our newsfeed for the latest
content from our friends and celebrities. It is hard to take time
to be silent. Silence makes us uncomfortable.

Marian theologians derive many meanings behind the apparition at Knock. But today, as we allow Our Lady to be a teacher
of prayer, she invites us to silent prayer. Do you have a place
where you can do this? Some people might do so in a special area
of their house or on their patio. Others might do it when they

walk; others at church. Find a place to spend a few minutes in silence. Put the phone away; better yet, turn it off! Clear your mind. And don't say anything. Just be still. Be silent. Know that God is God. And allow Him to speak to you. In the process, He might calm your mind, and in the silence, you might hear His whisper or experience His peace.

*Mary, teach me how to pray silently, so that I may contemplate the mysteries of Christ, hear His voice, and experience His peace.*

## Lenten Action

How long do you think you can practice silence today? Set aside ten minutes simply to be silent in God's presence. And if you are bold, turn the car radio off on your commute today or sometime this week and see what happens without the noise.

Thursday of the Fourth Week of Lent

# Meditating on the Word

*"My daughter, look at My Heart surrounded with thorns with which ungrateful men pierce it at every moment by their blasphemies and ingratitude. You, at least, try to console me, and say that I promise to assist at the hour of death, with all the graces necessary for salvation, all those who, on the first Saturday of five consecutive months go to confession, and receive Holy Communion, recite five decades of the Rosary and keep me company for a quarter of an hour while meditating on the mysteries of the Rosary, with the intention of making reparation to me."*

—Our Lady of Fatima

There are many ways of praying with the Sacred Scriptures. The monks taught a practice called *lectio divina*, or divine reading, in which a person reads a passage of Scripture, focuses on a word or phrase that resonates with him, and simply sits with the passage. The four steps of *lectio divina* are reading, meditating, praying (responding to the meditation) and contemplation, simply remaining in the moment with all that was received in prayer. St. Ignatius of Loyola, in his *Spiritual Exercises*, taught a method of praying with Scripture in which one imagines himself in the scene from a Gospel passage. Both are valid forms of praying with the Scriptures.

In a sense, to meditate on Scripture is to do what Luke tells us Mary did so often: to ponder the Word of God, to treasure it in our hearts. Mary, the pondering virgin, invites her children to pray as she prayed. When she taught the Five First Saturdays devotion to Sr. Lucia, she asked that we spend at least fifteen minutes meditating on the mysteries of the Rosary. (This is different from praying the Rosary, which Our Lady also asked us to do as part of the Five First Saturdays request.) Our Lady inivites devotees to open the Sacred Scriptures and read the mysteries, to ponder them, to pray with them. In that quiet reflection and meditation, one meditates on the Word of God.

Every encounter with the Word of God should change our lives. We know the stories. We have heard them so often. But every time we read or hear Scripture, something new might strike us. Every time, God wants to speak to us because His Word is living and true and pierces the heart. Each encounter with Scripture can be a moment of conversion, because, by meditating on the Word, we realize how we fall short of living that passage, or we discover God's invitation to a conversion of heart.

What role do the Scriptures play in your life? Mary had a great knowledge of the Scriptures, evident in her Magnificat, her song of praise at the Visitation, which quotes the song of Hannah. Do you read the Scriptures daily? If not, today is an opportunity to encounter the Word of God. Go find your Bible and see what God wants to say to you!

*Dear Blessed Mother, help me to know, meditate on, and live God's Sacred Word as you did during your life.*

## Lenten Action

Find the Gospel for the Fifth Sunday of Lent. You can do so by visiting usccb.org and clicking on the calendar on its website. Read the Gospel for this coming Sunday, and see what God wants to say to you. Pray like a monk with *lectio divina* or like St. Ignatius with imaginative prayer. When you go to Mass on Sunday, notice how more prepared you will be to hear the homily.

Friday of the Fourth Week of Lent

# Adoration

*Though your message was unspoken, still the truth in silence lies*
*as we gaze upon your vision, and the truth I try to find*
*here I stand with John the teacher, and with Joseph at your side*
*and I see the Lamb of God, on the Altar glorified.*

—Marian hymn describing the apparition at Knock

In Knock, Our Lady appeared with a lamb on an altar. This image should evoke in our minds an image of the Eucharist. Recall the words we hear at Mass day after day, Sunday after Sunday: "Lamb of God, you take away the sins of the world"; "Behold the Lamb of God." Jesus is the Lamb of God. He is the one sacrificed once and for all. The sacrifices of the Old Testament to atone for sins no longer need to be offered, because Jesus has satisfied for the sins of the world.

Every Mass we attend affords us the opportunity for adoration. After the priest says the words of Consecration, "This is my body.... This is the chalice of my blood," he elevates the Host or the chalice, and for a brief moment, we adore Jesus present in the Blessed Sacrament. How do you pray in that moment? Some people say silently, "My Lord and my God." Others might make an earnest prayer from their hearts or ask for an increase of love. They also might ask for forgiveness. It is a very powerful moment when God comes to earth through the sacrament.

As an extension of our act of adoration during the Elevation, we are also afforded the opportunity to adore Christ when the consecrated Host, in which He is present, is placed in a monstrance and set on an altar for an extended period for adoration. Some churches have what is called perpetual adoration, meaning that someone is always in the chapel praying to Jesus in the consecrated Host, keeping watch. Other parishes offer adoration once a week or once a month.

Adoration has always been a powerful time of prayer for me. Just as in my prayer before the tabernacle, I am able to bring to the Lord the many concerns and troubles of my life. But there is something special too. When Jesus is reposed in the tabernacle, I do not see Him, but when exposed in the monstrance, I am able to gaze at His Eucharistic presence and imagine Jesus gazing at me too. At some of the crisis moments of my life, I ran (actually drove) to an adoration chapel. One time I spent over two hours before the monstrance because I really needed to talk to Jesus. In that time, the Lord gave me a profound sense of peace and spoke to the depths of my heart. God wants to do the same thing for you. Try to adore Him in the Blessed Sacrament soon.

*Dear Blessed Mother, teach me how to adore Jesus as you adored Him.*

*Adoration*

## Lenten Action

Look for the nearest church that has adoration, either in a chapel or in the church at a scheduled time. Go and make a visit. If there isn't such a church close by, make an intentional moment of adoration this weekend at Mass, during the Elevation of the consecrated Host.

Saturday of the Fourth Week of Lent

# Litany of Loreto

*"Tell the girls of St. Stephen's to sing the Litany of the Blessed*
*Virgin in the church every evening, with the permission*
*of the Prior, and you will see that they will do it."*

—Our Lady of Laus

In most apparitions, the seers asked the heavenly lady to identify herself. Some visionaries were asked to do so by church authorities. St. Bernadette always referred to the woman as a beautiful lady until she gave her name as the Immaculate Conception. Adele Brise was told by her parish priest to ask, "In God's name, who are you, and what do you want of me?" Then Our Lady said, "I am the Queen of Heaven, who prays for the conversion of sinners." Other times, Our Lady told the visionaries that she would reveal her identity at a later time. The revealed name of Mary signifies something important and is used especially as the apparition is interpreted. Although many apparitions become known by their location—for example, Our Lady of Fatima and Our Lady of Lourdes—it is always important not to forget the revealed name.

Throughout the centuries of our Catholic Faith, the Mother of God has been honored under a variety of titles. These titles might relate to a role of Mary, such as virgin, mother, or queen;

others are devotional titles, such as Our Lady, Undoer of Knots. In 431, the Council of Ephesus affirmed Mary as the Theotokos, or God-bearer. Mary as the perpetual virgin has been saluted as "Virgin most prudent" or "Virgin most merciful." Jesus crowned Mary as Queen of Heaven and Earth, and we have ascribed many other regal titles for her. Some people get confused by all these titles. I've heard people ask if there are multiple Marys. There is one Mary, Mary of Nazareth, whose story and role in salvation history are told in the Gospels by the four evangelists. Because Mary loves the world so much, she has taken on many titles, which people invoke according to the nature of intercession needed. Some titles become affectionate ways for us to call upon our heavenly Mother.

When Our Lady appeared to Benoîte Rencurel in Laus, she asked her to teach the Litany of Loreto to the girls at St. Stephen's. Pope Leo XIII, who wrote many encyclicals on the Rosary during his pontificate, encouraged the recitation of the Litany of Loreto after the Rosary during the month of October. Today, being a Saturday, a day traditionally attributed to Marian devotion, it seems appropriate for us to ask the intercession of Our Lady. As we pray the Litany of Loreto, we do so in fulfillment of Our Lady's request to Benoîte.

*Dear Blessed Mother, as I call upon you by various names and titles throughout my life, I ask you never to forget my name, especially at the hour of my death.*

## Lenten Action

Pray the Litany of Loreto. As you pray each title of Mary, pause for a second, and ask what that title might mean.

After the litany, consider which title of Mary is
vorite. What does that title of Mary mean to you. __
another favorite title of Mary that is more devotional and
not in the Litany of Loreto? What do you like about it?
Consider sharing about that devotion on social media.

*Litany of Loreto*

Lord have mercy.
*Christ have mercy.*
Lord have mercy.
Christ hear us.
*Christ graciously hear us.*

God the Father of Heaven, *have mercy on us.*
God the Son, Redeemer of the world, *have mercy on us.*
God the Holy Spirit, *have mercy on us.*
Holy Trinity, one God, *have mercy on us.*

Holy Mary, *pray for us.*
Holy Mother of God, *pray for us.*
Holy Virgin of virgins, *pray for us.*
Mother of Christ, *pray for us.*
Mother of the Church, *pray for us.*
Mother of divine grace, *pray for us.*
Mother most pure, *pray for us.*
Mother most chaste, *pray for us.*
Mother inviolate, *pray for us.*
Mother undefiled, *pray for us.*
Mother most amiable, *pray for us.*
Mother most admirable, *pray for us.*
Mother of good counsel, *pray for us.*
Mother of our Creator, *pray for us.*

# A Lenten Journey with Mother Mary

Mother of our Savior, *pray for us.*
Mother of mercy, *pray for us.*
Virgin most prudent, *pray for us.*
Virgin most venerable, *pray for us.*
Virgin most renowned, *pray for us.*
Virgin most powerful, *pray for us.*
Virgin most merciful, *pray for us.*
Virgin most faithful, *pray for us.*
Mirror of justice, *pray for us.*
Seat of wisdom, *pray for us.*
Cause of our joy, *pray for us.*
Spiritual vessel, *pray for us.*
Vessel of honor, *pray for us.*
Singular vessel of devotion, *pray for us.*
Mystical rose, *pray for us.*
Tower of David, *pray for us.*
Tower of ivory, *pray for us.*
House of gold, *pray for us.*
Ark of the covenant, *pray for us.*
Gate of Heaven, *pray for us.*
Morning star, *pray for us.*
Health of the sick, *pray for us.*
Refuge of sinners, *pray for us.*
Comfort of the afflicted, *pray for us.*
Help of Christians, *pray for us.*
Queen of angels, *pray for us.*
Queen of patriarchs, *pray for us.*
Queen of prophets, *pray for us.*
Queen of apostles, *pray for us.*
Queen of martyrs, *pray for us.*
Queen of confessors, *pray for us.*

Queen of virgins, *pray for us.*
Queen of all saints, *pray for us.*
Queen conceived without original sin, *pray for us.*
Queen assumed into Heaven, *pray for us.*
Queen of the most holy Rosary, *pray for us.*
Queen of families, *pray for us.*
Queen of peace, *pray for us.*

Lamb of God, who takest away the sins of the world,
    *spare us, O Lord.*
Lamb of God, who takest away the sins of the world,
    *graciously hear us, O Lord.*
Lamb of God, who takest away the sins of the world,
    *have mercy on us.*
Pray for us, O holy Mother of God.
    *That we may be made worthy of the promises of Christ.*

*Let us pray.* Grant, we beseech thee, O Lord God, that we, Your servants, may enjoy perpetual health of mind and body; and by the intercession of the Blessed Mary, ever virgin, may be delivered from present sorrow, and obtain eternal joy. Through Christ our Lord. Amen.

Fifth Week of Lent

# Healing

Many spiritual writers today tell us that what the world needs most is healing. We have all been wounded—hurt by others, hurt by sin. We also need healing because of disease and sickness. And we know of others who are in need healing. Healing was central to many of Our Lady's messages. This week, we will pray for healing for ourselves and others, asking Our Lady to obtain the graces for which we ask.

# Everyone Knows Someone
# Who Needs Healing

*"Go to the spring, drink of it,
and wash yourself there."*

—Our Lady of Lourdes

Those familiar with the apparitions at Lourdes know that the site is known for miraculous healing and a spring of water. Millions of people have visited Lourdes to bathe in those waters and pray at the grotto. They even bring the water home with them in little bottles that they buy. I am one of those pilgrims.

In my parish work, I encounter many people who are sick. I've given Lourdes water to a young girl with stomach issues, a woman dying of a brain tumor, and a young husband and father who was dying of cancer. The young man's children blessed him nightly with the water. I've helped a Catholic school teacher pray with a child whose foot was infected. The young boy stepped on a pitchfork, and it went through his foot. After the initial emergency visit, the foot became inflamed and infected. The teacher, with the class, surrounded the student and invoked Mary's intercession for healing. I was out of town at the time, and upon my return,

nessage from the boy's father to call him when
ssumed the worst — that the boy had to have
lled, and our conversation was nothing of the
᠁, the doctors didn't understand how his foot became better so quickly. The young boy believed it was the miraculous power of the Lourdes water. As the story spread to others, another young boy whose growth plate was broken because of a sports injury asked me to bless his leg with the same water. A week or two later, he was back to playing baseball. Whether or not the water facilitated these healings remains to be seen, but at the very least, it increased faith and gave greater confidence in God during difficult moments.

These people were in need of healing and comfort, and that's what the Lourdes water helped to provide. Today the Order of Malta brings sick people to Lourdes for them to experience healing, comfort, and peace. Sometimes the healing we ask for, pray for, and want isn't the healing God will give us. No matter what, God always gives grace when we choose spiritual things.

There are people in your life who need healing, too. They could be family members or friends, coworkers or strangers. Their healing need might be physical, or it could be spiritual, emotional, or psychological. Today let us ask Our Lady, Health of the Sick, to pray for those we love who need God's healing touch.

*Mary, Health of the Sick, through your prayers, you have obtained healing for many. Today I ask you to pray for (insert names), that God will heal them in the ways they need.*

## Lenten Action

You might not have access to Lourdes water, but every church has holy water. Bless yourself and your family with holy water, and invoke Mary's intercession for healing. God knows the healing we need. Let Him take care of it.

Monday of the Fifth Week of Lent

# Spiritual Reparation

*"Sacrifice yourselves for sinners, and say many times, especially*
*when you make some sacrifice: O Jesus, it is for love of*
*You, for the conversion of sinners, and in reparation for the*
*sins committed against the Immaculate Heart of Mary."*

—Our Lady of Fatima

In Our Lady's apparitions at Fatima, she requested reparation for sin. Jesus, when He revealed His Sacred Heart, also requested reparation. Sin wounds. It wounds us, and it wounds others. The wounds caused by sin require healing. One way that healing occurs is through our acts of reparation, by which our prayers and sacrifices repair damage and hurt. Sometimes that healing can be difficult, or the sins and hurt caused to others cannot be healed by reaching out to them, because we don't know how to contact them. That was the case for me. I chose to offer my pain for the healing of the hurt I caused another individual.

Some stories we share are embarrassing. That's true for this story of reparation. Bullying has been an age-old problem. Unfortunately, I was a bully in this instance. One day when I was in fourth grade, I made fun of another student in the schoolyard. After a few exchanges of taunting, this boy swung his backpack

, hit me in the mouth, and chipped one of my front teeth. family didn't have dental insurance, so I just lived with that chipped tooth and reluctantly smiled. In high school, that chipped tooth shattered one day, and I immediately went to the dentist. The dentist did the best he could to repair the damage by building a temporary composite tooth, but because of the overcrowding in my mouth, the tooth was built crooked.

Every time I went to the dentist, he told me that I had to do something about that tooth, but a permanent solution could not happen until I got braces to align my teeth. As a twenty-eight-year-old, I finally went to the orthodontist because I knew the temporary tooth wouldn't survive forever. I had the braces installed, and to bring the composite tooth into alignment, a button hook was necessary. The few days after that button was installed were painful. I could feel every tug and throb in my tooth. As I sat before the Blessed Sacrament one evening during that painful time, I thought of the reason I needed those braces—because I taunted that boy so many years ago. I don't know what happened to him. He moved away from the school district within a year or two of the incident. What I do know is that my sin could have caused him harm in some way. Praying before the Lord, I offered every ache, tug, and throb to Jesus for that young man, asking the Lord to grant him healing in whatever way he needed and to provide for him in the circumstances of his life. I hope that my prayer and pain, offered as reparation for my sins, brought him healing and grace.

*Dear Blessed Mother, I respond to your request and wish to make reparation for my sins. Lord Jesus, receive my prayer and offering and bring healing to someone whom I have hurt.*

## Lenten Action

Spend a few moments reflecting on your life and your relationships. Is there someone whom you have fallen out of touch with who requires healing because of your hurtful words or actions? Resolve today to make an act of self-denial, asking God to flood that person's soul with healing graces and mercy.

# For Those with Debilitating Diseases

*"This spring is reserved for all the nations — to relieve the sick."*

—Our Lady of Banneux

Even though we began this week of prayer for healing by praying for those who are sick, it is important to realize that there are many types of sickness out there. There are those who have cancer or suffer the effects of strokes. Others were diagnosed with diabetes at a very young age and have struggled with it throughout their lives. That was the case for my mother.

My mom's diabetes began to affect her more in her late forties. Blockages in veins led to amputations in her foot, toe by toe, and at some point, she would require a leg amputation. I knew my mom wouldn't do well as an amputee, and I prayed daily that God would miraculously dissolve the clot her in leg. I learned about Fr. Solanus Casey, the saintly Capuchin from Detroit who was going to be beatified later in 2017. I read a biography of him and discovered that he also faced the possibility of amputation during a hospitalization, although it didn't happen. I decided to entrust my mother to the intercession of Solanus Casey, and I heeded another request of his. He told those who asked for his prayers that they should read the book *The Mystical City of God* by

# A Lenten Journey with Mother Mary

Venerable Maria of Agreda. Many who did so received the grace they desired. After I prayed for Father Solanus's intercession, I would always read a few pages from *The Mystical City of God*. My mother died a few months after I began this devotion, but as I preached in the funeral homily, I believe that God answered my prayers; because she died, my mother never had to have her leg amputated, and that is what I prayed for.

When Our Lady appeared to a young girl named Mariette Becco in Banneux, Belgium, she took Mariette to a spring of water and said, "This spring is reserved for all the nations — to relieve the sick." In our prayer, we can ask Mary to bring relief to those we know who are sick. It might be to relieve the symptoms they currently face or to bring relief so they suffer no more. For my mother, I realized that relief came through death, and I had to accept it. Once I did, I was better able to cope and to mourn because I realized that Our Lady accomplished what she came to do in Banneux.

*Virgin of the Poor please relieve the suffering of those who are sick.*

## Lenten Action

How might you bring relief to someone who is sick? Through words or a kind gesture? Cooking a meal? Running an errand? You can provide the relief someone needs.

Wednesday of the Fifth Week of Lent

# For Those Struggling with Infertility

*"O Mary, conceived without sin, pray for*
*us who have recourse to thee."*

—Our Lady of the Miraculous Medal

Scripture recounts stories of couples unable to conceive. Apocryphal accounts relate that the parents of Mary, Joachim and Anne, were blessed with the miraculous conception of the Blessed Virgin. One of the intentions of my priestly heart is for couples who are unable to conceive. I invoke the intercession of Our Lady of the Milk (also Our Lady of La Leche and Our Lady of Good Delivery). I first encountered the devotion in the Holy Land at the Milk Grotto and heard the testimony of the Franciscan custodian of the shrine, who shared about countless miracle babies. There is a shrine in Saint Augustine, Florida, that couples visit to pray before the image of the Nursing Madonna. Again, there are many testimonies of the La Leche babies and the fruit of the pilgrims' devotion and Mary's prayers.

Mary called herself the Immaculate Conception when she appeared in Lourdes, France. Only four years earlier, the Holy Father had dogmatically defined Mary's preservation from original sin. If we consider who Mary is and grant that her parents struggled to conceive and were gifted with the child Mary, and that God acted so powerfully in her life to foresee the merits of Christ, then we can understand how she obtains the grace of these miraculous conceptions for those seeking it. Even though many couples do conceive, many do not. And then we ask for the grace of adoption for them, so they might form families of their own.

There is a certain healing that is needed for a couple in this situation—yes, a healing of the physical barrier to conception, but also an emotional healing. Carrying the weight of infertility causes struggles within a person and even within a marriage. Spiritual healing might also be necessary, because the couple might question and doubt why God would not allow them to conceive. There might be anger or resentment toward God. Today let us ask for Mary's fertile prayers as we entrust to her all those unable to conceive. May God give them the grace of physical healing or the healing of accepting and loving an adopted child.

*Mary, you are the Immaculate Conception. You who were spared the stain of original sin and conceived Jesus by the power of the Holy Spirit, please intercede for couples struggling to conceive for the grace and healing they need.*

## Lenten Action
In the spirit of almsgiving, donate diapers to a local pregnancy center.

Thursday of the Fifth Week of Lent

# For the Healing of Marriages

*" 'The final battle between the Lord and the kingdom of
Satan will be about Marriage and the Family.' Don't
be afraid, because whoever works for the sanctity of
Marriage and the Family will always be fought against and
opposed in every way, because this is the decisive issue.
Nevertheless, Our Lady has already crushed his head."*

—Sr. Lucia dos Santos

A Catholic News Agency article reported this quotation attributed to Sr. Lucia from a private correspondence received by
Cardinal Carlo Caffarra. In the third millennium, these words
might seem true if you look at the state of the family throughout
the world: fatherless homes, single-parent households, divorce,
the redefinition of marriage. All of these things seem to attack
the validity of the biblical teaching about marriage: the two,
man and woman, becoming one flesh.

Some regard this quote as a prophecy. It doesn't necessarily
come from Our Lady herself but from the fruit of Our Lady's
visionary. Sr. Lucia was a woman of prayer who lived her days
fulfilling the message Our Lady gave to her. It was from the fruit
of this prayer that Sr. Lucia spoke about marriage and family.

# A Lenten Journey with Mother Mary

During her lifetime, she saw the institution of the family struggling. St. John Paul II and Pope Francis have written about the family and how the Church can better serve families.

During this week focused on healing, we pray for families, realizing that there is a lot of healing for which we need to pray. In families where spouses no longer love each other, healing is needed. Spouses who struggle with alcohol or pornography addictions need healing. Pray intensely for anyone you know who needs to break free from addiction. Offer sacrifices for them. Ask Our Lady, Undoer of Knots, to pray for couples whose marriages are broken. This devotion has been efficacious with broken marriages. Some spouses might need healing of their memories, from hurts and offenses they've committed. Pray that they may receive the healing of forgiving their spouses or forgiving themselves.

Sr. Lucia might be right about the battle between hell and the family. When the family is destroyed, chaos and disorder happen. Let us pray for healing so we might have the same confidence Sr. Lucia had, that Our Lady has already crushed the devil's head.

*Our Lady, Undoer of Knots, untie the knots in troubled marriages and unite spouses again in love.*

## Lenten Action

Pray a Rosary for a couple you know who is going through a difficult time in their marriage, or pray a Rosary in thanksgiving for the blessings of your married life.

Friday of the Fifth Week of Lent

# For Healing for Our Country

*"A river of blood, people who were killing each other,*
*abandoned corpses with no one to bury them, trees*
*all in flames, bodies without their heads."*

—Our Lady of Kibeho

Many of Our Lady's apparitions, such as those at Fatima, Banneux, and Beauraing, occurred during wartime. The apparitions at Fatima and Kibeho prophesied even worse events. Our Lady is concerned about peace, which we prayed for earlier in our Lenten pilgrimage.

People need healing after war. Some people may hold serious grudges against other countries, especially if someone they loved perished in battle or as a bystander.

Countries also experience the divisiveness of politics, pitting families against each other and fostering hatred for others. People need healing from this ill will.

Countries and their inhabitants need to experience healing from the effects of racism. The bishops in the United States issued a 2018 pastoral statement on the topic. Healing needs to begin on an individual level. Those who feel animosity toward others must look within and try to find and root out the cause.

And, of course, those who have experienced or still experience racism need healing from the sufferings racism causes.

Countries themselves need healing because of corporate sin. The song "America the Beautiful" has a very powerful line: "God mend thine every flaw." Every time I sing that song, I think of the scourge of abortion and other offenses against human life and dignity. Our country needs healing from these sins and their effects.

*Queen of Peace, obtain healing for our country and for all its citizens.*

## Lenten Action

Are there more ways our country needs healing? Say a prayer from your heart for our country, asking God to bless our land.

Saturday of the Fifth Week of Lent

# For Healing of Our Broken Hearts

*When Jesus saw his mother and the disciple there whom*
*he loved, he said to his mother, "Woman, behold, your*
*son." Then he said to the disciple, "Behold, your mother."*
*And from that hour the disciple took her into his home.*

—John 19:26–27

"I allow you to become broken, so that I can put the pieces back together." These are the words Jesus said to me as I prayed in an adoration chapel after I had hit rock bottom in my life. In the midst of my brokenness, Jesus was going to put me back together.

Throughout life, our hearts might be broken, and they will need mending. We might have a broken heart over a breakup in a relationship. Whether it was a friendship or someone we loved deeply, we need healing to be able to move on. A broken heart might result from harsh words people have said to us—people we believed were our friends but who disappointed us. How do we find healing to restore such a friendship or move beyond it? When our dreams are dashed—whether it's a life goal or our career—our hearts break. When you lose your sense of direction, where do you turn so that your heart can be mended?

# A Lenten Journey with Mother Mary

The Scriptures tell us that the Lord heals the brokenhearted and binds all their wounds (see Ps. 147:3). In these most difficult moments we turn to God, and in Him we find the source of our strength and healing. In one sense, the heart of Mary was wounded or broken—not because of sin, because she was sinless. Her heart was broken because of the sorrows that filled her life and the world; broken because the Holy Innocents were slaughtered by Herod, who wanted to put Jesus to death; broken because she had to flee into Egypt for safety; broken as she stood beneath the Cross of Jesus, seeing Him die. But Jesus heals her broken heart. From the Cross, out of compassion, Jesus says, "Woman, behold your son." Jesus does not want to abandon His Mother. He does not want to leave her broken and alone. Even from the Cross, as Jesus brought healing and salvation to the world, He cared for the most important woman in His life, making sure that her motherly heart would be healed with the help of John. God wants to heal our broken hearts. He wants to put the pieces back together. Give Him permission.

*Dear Blessed Mother, obtain from your Son the healing of our hearts, that what is broken might become whole.*

## Lenten Action

Pray about how you can heal your heart or someone's heart. If you know you hurt someone, reach out to that person, and offer a kind word. If someone has hurt you, pray that you might be able to forgive that person.

# Holy Week

Lent is nearly over. During the last several weeks, we have listened to Our Lady and her motherly advice and wisdom. In these last days of Lent, which we call Holy Week, we will focus on Our Lady's role in the Passion of Christ, especially her suffering. We will journey with her, so that she will not be alone, and we can bring her comfort, and she can console us also. And let us accompany her from the Cross to the grave so that we may be with her when she receives the news that Jesus is risen!

Palm Sunday

# Are You Ready for Your Pilgrimage?

*Although the Blessed Virgin was carried away fainting*
*after the sad meeting with her Son loaded with His*
*Cross, yet she soon recovered consciousness, for*
*love, and the ardent desire of seeing Him once more,*
*imparted to her a supernatural feeling of strength.*

—Anne Catherine Emmerich, *The Dolorous*
*Passion of Our Lord Jesus Christ*

In the early years of Christianity and now for centuries, Christians have gone to the Holy Land to see the places important in the life of Christ. Pilgrims visit Nazareth, where the Holy Family lived. They visit Bethlehem and venerate the spot where Jesus was born. They visit places where Jesus taught, healed, and performed His miracles. And, of course, they visit Calvary, where Christ died. They venerate the anointing stone and the empty tomb of Jesus.

Our annual experience of Holy Week is a pilgrimage. We become witnesses of Christ's Passion and participate in the Passion narrative. At the beginning of Holy Week, we are there as Christ enters Jerusalem to the waving of palm branches and the singing of "hosanna." We will be there on Holy Thursday, as Christ institutes the Eucharist at the Last Supper and washes the feet of His disciples. At the conclusion of Holy Thursday, we will enter the garden, and pray with Jesus at the altar of repose. On Good Friday, we will visit Calvary, and stand with John and Mary as Christ dies on the Cross. On Easter Sunday, we will run with the disciples to the empty tomb and see what Mary Magdalene proclaimed: that Jesus' body is not there.

Jesus was on a pilgrimage throughout His life. He came from Heaven to earth to die for us and to lift our human nature to the heavenly realm. The last days of His life were a pilgrimage to Calvary. His pilgrimage is our pilgrimage. Our pilgrimage is not only to the earthly Jerusalem but to the heavenly Jerusalem. As we follow Jesus this Holy Week and witness these events, we hope to follow Him, just as His Mother must have followed Him along each step.

Those who go on a pilgrimage prepare themselves. If it is a walking pilgrimage, for instance, they prepare through daily exercise. Pilgrims also have to pack their suitcases, and they might read a book to learn more about the places they will visit. Mary must have prepared herself for her pilgrimage to Jerusalem. How will you prepare for your Holy Week pilgrimage? Will you practice walking by praying the Stations? What will you pack in your spiritual suitcase? What will you read?

*Dear Blessed Mother, help me to prepare for my pilgrimage of Holy Week as I walk by your side during Christ's Passion.*

## Lenten Action

Regardless of how your Lenten resolutions have gone, resolve for this week to take on a Lenten discipline.

Monday of Holy Week

# Experiencing Holy Week with Our Lady

*Our place of safety will be beneath the mantle of the holy
Mother of God. By our silent witness in prayer, we give
ourselves and others an accounting for the hope that is within.*

—Pope Francis, Palm Sunday 2019

Yesterday our Sunday Mass commemorated Jesus' entry into Jerusalem on a donkey and the people greeting Him with "Hosanna in the highest." We heard the Passion narrative and all that Jesus experienced on the way to Calvary: left alone in the garden while the apostles slept; betrayed by Judas; denied by Peter; abandoned by the other apostles, who scattered. During this Holy Week, let us imagine Mary as she journeyed with Jesus. Let us be her companion so that we may console and comfort her.

Let us pause today and consider how Mary must have felt as a witness to all of this. I can only imagine that Jesus brought His disciples, His closest friends, home with Him from time to time. The Gospels tell us that Mary went looking for Jesus one day to see where He was (Mark 3:31–35). St. Maximus the Confessor believed that Mary would have followed Jesus during His public ministry. Suffice it to say, Mary was close to the apostles. She is called the Queen of Apostles. She was a mother to them. Her motherly heart must have been broken — broken because she witnessed her Son in so much pain and because those who loved Him were not there in His final moments.

Mary remained faithful, despite witnessing all of these things. She watched Jesus in agony as she stood beneath the Cross. She later consoled the apostles who came to her, one by one, for her motherly counsel and love.

As we meditate on Mary's sorrow for Jesus and the apostles this week, let us realize that she experiences sorrow because of us. This is why she has often come to the world, because we forget what Jesus did. It's why she asked the children at Kibeho to pray the Seven Sorrows Rosary, so that we might not forget her suffering. Let us enter into this Holy Week with Mary, asking her to obtain many graces for us as we contemplate her Son's Passion, so we might not forget, so we will not break her heart.

*Sorrowful Mother, I want to walk with you during this Holy Week. Allow me to experience it through your eyes and understand what you suffered. May I never take for granted all that Jesus did for me.*

## Lenten Action

Imagine what you would say to Mary if you were one of the apostles. Then realize that you are saying that to her because of your sins. Then pray the Hail Holy Queen.

Tuesday of Holy Week

# Participating in Christ's Passion

*Standing by the cross of Jesus were his mother and his mother's*
*sister, Mary, the wife of Clopas, and Mary of Magdala.*

—John 19:25

Mary stood at the foot of the Cross. This is why many saints call her an associate in the work of redemption. The Second Vatican Council's Dogmatic Constitution *Lumen Gentium* says this about Mary's participation in Christ's Passion: Mary "faithfully persevered in her union with her Son unto the cross, where she stood, in keeping with the divine plan (cf. John 19:25), grieving exceedingly with her only begotten Son, uniting herself with a maternal heart with His sacrifice, and lovingly consenting to the immolation of this Victim which she herself had brought forth" (no. 58). Mary's presence at the Cross allowed her a participation in Christ's saving action as she united her suffering to that of Jesus. Mary experienced this participation earlier when she consented to be the Mother of God. By her affirmation, she ushered in this moment of salvation. By her Immaculate Conception, Mary had received the merits of the Cross and was preserved from Original Sin, thereby allowing her to participate intimately and jointly in this salvific work of Christ.

# A Lenten Journey with Mother Mary

Our Catholic tradition bestows value on sacrifice, calling it efficacious when offered for an intention. You might have heard the phrase "offer it up" as a way to give meaning to some suffering you were experiencing. Some saints freely choose to take suffering on themselves for a greater purpose.

Blessed Chiara Luce Badano (1971–1990), an Italian teenager, is an example. When she was hospitalized with terminal bone cancer, Chiara she refused morphine because she wanted to identify with the sufferings of Christ. She wanted to enter into the Passion of Jesus and offer her suffering for the world. This is called redemptive suffering, which means that a person can bring meaning to suffering by offering it for some greater good, a prayer intention, and so forth. By attaching a spiritual meaning to sacrifice, we participate in Christ's Passion to a small extent, but even more, we ensure that no suffering is in vain.

Mary's suffering was a true participation in the Cross, and most certainly she turned it into a prayer for those who betrayed Jesus and for all of us, realizing that His sacrifice would atone for the sins of all generations. In imitation of Mary, not only on this day of Holy Week, but often, choose to share in Christ's Passion. Offer your suffering and allow it to become redemptive and spiritually efficacious for the Church and the world.

*Mary, just as you stood by Jesus in His Passion, stand by me in the moments of suffering in my life.*

## Lenten Action

What pain or suffering are you able to offer for the salvation of souls today? Don't let your suffering go to waste.

Wednesday of Holy Week

# Mary's Tears

*The sitting Madonna with her head in her hands*
*is the unspoken message of La Salette.*

When was the last time you cried? Was it because someone you loved died or because someone said something hurtful? Were they tears of joy from recalling a happy memory? Or maybe they were even tears of great sorrow for something you did. During this Holy Week, Mary's tears can be a subject of our meditation. Pilgrims visit the Milk Grotto in the Holy Land because a pious tradition says that a few drops of Mary's milk fell to the ground in that place. Similarly, pilgrims walk the Via Dolorosa, where, instead of milk, Mary's tears surely fell to the ground as she followed her Son to Calvary.

In Our Catholic tradition, some claim to have witnessed miraculous phenomena, such as weeping statues of the Blessed Virgin. In Catholic artwork over the centuries, Mary has been depicted as weeping. In her apparitions at La Salette, Mary wept over the sins of the local people.

Mary's tears intensified during her Holy Week experience. Imagine her hearing the crowds shout, "Crucify Him! Crucify Him!" Imagine Jesus' scourging at the pillar. Perhaps Mary went to wipe up His blood, which stained the ground. The tears she must have shed! As she stood beneath the Cross, hearing the mocking crowds, watching her Son suffer, she must have cried. As Jesus entrusted her to John and later took His last breath, she surely cried. Holding the lifeless body of Jesus in her arms and at the tomb, she must have shed tears.

The tears of Mary, as the Mother of Jesus and of us, are still as real today. Our yearly observance of Holy Week presents to us again the tears of Mary. But we can also consider her tears throughout the history of the Church. In the early Church, as the first believers in her Son were martyred, she mourned their deaths. During times in which heresy and false teaching were spread, Mary, even though in Heaven, was sad for the pilgrim Church on earth. Even today, all the division that exists among believers must bring sorrow to the heart of Mary. The sins of society and individuals are also cause for Mary's tears, as they were at La Salette; surely, she still sheds tears today over so much evil.

As we begin the Triduum tomorrow, let us walk with Our Lady in our prayer. Cry with her and comfort her with your prayers. And let us strive never to be the reason for her to cry again.

*Sorrowful Mother, I want to walk with you throughout these next days. As I witness your tears, please obtain from your Son the grace that I may never cause you sorrow again.*

## Lenten Action

St. Bridget of Sweden promoted a devotion to meditating on Our Lady's tears. She recommended praying seven Hail Marys in honor of Mary's tears during the Seven Sorrows.

Holy Thursday

# Our Lady of the Sacristy

Lanthorn aloft, the Mother crossed the room,
Lingered a little where He last had sat,
Shepherd to flock of twelve
Already stirred by breath upon the wind
Of nearing wolves.
A chalice stood where He had laid it down,
Taken from John,
The very first to drink,
The last to hold it for a second to his heart.
One drop of wine that was no longer wine
Deep in its crystal throat
She carried to her lips,
Drinking it down,
Who once had given blood to fill the veins
Of God within Her.
Then reverently she wrapped it in her veil,
Hiding it in a cabinet that stood
Waiting to be the first Repository.

—Fr. Daniel Lord, *The Song of the Rosary*

# A Lenten Journey with Mother Mary

Fr. Daniel Lord (1888–1955), an American Jesuit and the author of more than ninety books, three hundred pamphlets, and numerous articles, plays, and songs, wrote a very beautiful book of poetry and meditations on Christ's life intertwined with the Rosary mysteries, titled *The Song of the Rosary*. Fr. Lord situates the excerpt above within his meditation for the Agony in the Garden. He sets the scene. It is after the Last Supper, and the disciples are now singing their hymns and going to the Garden. Mary is close by that Upper Room and enters after all have left. It is as if Mary is the first sacristan. She cleans everything and puts it away. In the prayerful imagination of Fr. Lord, Mary finds a chalice containing a drop of the wine turned into the Precious Blood, which she consumes. For Mary, this is her first Holy Communion, but it would not be her last, as she celebrated with the disciples the Breaking of the Bread, doing what Jesus did on the night before He died, in obedience to His command: Do this in remembrance of me.

As we prepare to celebrate this Holy Thursday, the night of the Lord's Supper and the institution of the Holy Eucharist, Fr. Lord affords us a few things to think, meditate, and pray about. In a meditation in his book *Christ in Me*, Fr. Lord proposes that Mary prepared the Upper Room. She put out the tablecloth and prepared the room for Jesus and His apostles. If Mary prepared the room for the supper, we, as guests, should prepare ourselves in some way. The next time you go to Mass, whether it is tonight for Holy Thursday or on Sunday for Easter, make an act of preparation. Calm your mind, heart, and soul, and consider what you are about to experience. Think of Mary's reception of the drop of Christ's Blood. How did she pray afterward? When you receive Holy Communion, do you make an act of thanksgiving? Mary, as a recipient of Holy Communion, teaches us that we ought to prepare for Mass and make a thanksgiving after Holy Communion. The next time you go to Mass, don't go through the motions, but be intentional about everything you do. In this, you will find greater meaning in our Eucharistic celebrations.

*Dear Blessed Mother, as you received your Son in the Holy Eucharist from the hands of the apostles, give me the same disposition you had. Show me what it means to prepare, and teach me how to make a Eucharistic thanksgiving.*

## Lenten Action

Before you go to Mass, consider how you will prepare, whom you want to pray for (your Mass intention), and how you will spend a few moments meditating or thanking God for the gift of the Holy Eucharist.

Good Friday

# Don't Give Up

*At the Cross her station keeping,*
*Stood the mournful Mother weeping,*
*Close to Jesus to the last.*

— "Stabat Mater"

Mary was faithful. She journeyed with Jesus during Holy Week. She met Him on the way to Calvary. And there, with John, Mary of Clopas, and Mary Magdalene, she stood at the foot of the Cross. The words of the "Stabat Mater" tell us: "At the Cross her station keeping, stood the mournful Mother weeping, close to Jesus to the last." This stanza of that beautiful hymn reminds us that Mary stayed by Jesus' side to the bitter end. Imagine her pain as a mother, watching her beloved Son die on the Cross. It might have been easy for Mary to give up and question how this was part of God's plan for salvation. But her faith was persistent. She didn't give up. Instead, she united herself to Jesus on the Cross.

We might want to give up on something — maybe a job or a project or a friendship, or even life itself. As a person involved in academia, sometimes I want to give up on papers I am writing. I even thought about dropping a class altogether in the final weeks because I wasn't sure I could continue and write the requisite research paper. And believe it or not, I abandoned this Lenten book a few days before the deadline.

Discouragement can get the best of us. Mary could have been discouraged. But she held fast to all the teachings of Jesus. She maintained her faith. In those moments when we want to give up, let us remind ourselves of Mary's example. Remember Good Friday and how she stayed by Jesus. We might want to give up on God, faith, or prayer. And this might be easy to do. Mary's example encourages us never to give up on God.

It might be a bit difficult to relate to Mary, because she was a perfect human being by virtue of the Immaculate Conception. She had perfect faith. Our discouragement should make us consider what causes us to want to give up. Maybe it is fear, loneliness, abandonment, or a lack of faith. Our struggles can become opportunities to exercise faith in God. We can ask, "Where are You leading me?" "How does this accomplish Your will?" On this Good Friday, as we mourn Jesus' death, as we stand by Mary at the foot of the Cross, let us draw strength for the struggles we will face in life. Jesus did not give up on the Cross. Mary remained faithful to the end. May God find us always faithful like Mary.

*Sorrowful Mother, I want to be like you, faithful to the end.*

## Lenten Action

Attend a Good Friday service, or, if you are unable, pray the Stations of the Cross, or read the Passion narrative in one of the Gospels or online. As you do so, consider the many times it would have been easy for Jesus or Mary to give up on the Way of the Cross.

Holy Saturday

# Remembering Our Beloved Dead

*It was toward eleven o'clock at night when the Blessed Virgin,*
*incited by irrepressible feelings of love, arose, wrapped a gray*
*cloak around her, and left the house quite alone. . . . I saw*
*her go first to the house of Caiaphas, and then to the palace*
*of Pilate, which was at a great distance off; I watched her*
*through the whole of her solitary journey along that part which*
*had been trodden by her Son, loaded with His heavy Cross;*
*she stopped at every place where our Savior had suffered.*

—Anne Catherine Emmerich, *The Dolorous*
*Passion of Our Lord Jesus Christ*

Where do you think Mary spent the hours after Jesus' death?
Whom did she spend them with? We don't know the answer
to these questions, but we could speculate. Maybe she stayed at
the tomb of Jesus, crying and lamenting His death. Or maybe
she stayed in the Upper Room, and later rewalked the path
of Jesus' Passion on that Saturday afternoon, arriving to visit
Jesus' tomb.

What have you done after a loved one has died? How have
you grieved? I'm sure that Mary remembered her life with Jesus
and treasured all those memories in her heart. She wanted to

revisit the places of importance in Jesus' Passion. I like to believe she walked the Way of the Cross many times.

One day, I picked up two fish plates from a local grocery store and brought them to my mother's house, and we ate supper together. When I drove by that store after my mother died, I remembered that experience and wanted to relive it.

My mother also loved going to the Wisconsin State Fair, and so, the first year after her death, I decided to go and experience the state fair and try to understand why she loved it so much. I am sure there are many customs that you observe as a way to remember a loved one who has died. Someone I know planned to take her kids fishing on the anniversary of their father's death, because they had enjoyed fishing with their dad, and it seemed appropriate to remember him in that way. When we relive such experiences to remember our loved ones, we are doing what Mary did. She mourned Jesus' death and never forgot their many experiences together. Remember your beloved dead by reliving experiences you had with them.

*Dear Blessed Mother, help me to mourn the death of Jesus as you did. Please console me as I mourn the death of Jesus and of my loved ones who have died.*

## Lenten Action

Visit a cemetery and pray at the grave of a loved one or a friend. Or do something that will help you to remember a loved one who has died.

# Easter Octave

From Good Friday to the Sunday after Easter, many Catholics pray the Divine Mercy Novena, which comes to us from the diary of St. Faustina Kowalska, a Polish mystic and visionary who received many apparitions of Jesus. Jesus asked her to have painted the familiar image of Divine Mercy, with rays coming forth from Jesus' heart and the words "Jesus, I trust in You" etched at the bottom. During this week, we will confront the doubts we might have and pray for greater faith and trust in God.

Easter Sunday

# Mary's Encounter with the Risen Christ

*Nevertheless, the immaculate mother was inseparable from the*
*tomb, and she was watching and listening to everything that*
*was happening and being said. She saw the great earthquake*
*that woke the first fruits of those who have fallen asleep and*
*put the guards to sleep and rolled away the stone, and then*
*the waking of the guards again and their entry into the city.*
*All this the women who had gone and come back again were*
*not able to see, but the blessed mother of the Lord, seized*
*by love of her son and standing inseparably at the tomb,*
*was a witness to everything until she saw even his glorious*
*Resurrection. . . . Only the immaculate mother of the Lord*
*standing there knew everything. And because of this, she received*
*the good news of the Resurrection before everyone else.*

—Maximus the Confessor, *The Life of the Virgin*, par. 92

Did Jesus appear to His Blessed Mother first after the Resurrection? The general consensus is yes. St. Ignatius of Loyola proposes this in his *Spiritual Exercises*. St. John Paul II believed it too. There is no official teaching on the subject. You are left to believe what you wish. Such an appearance is not recorded in the Sacred Scriptures because it is not necessary for our salvation. But it has been the subject of pious musing and theological debates. Those who contend that Jesus didn't appear to his Blessed Mother first suggest two reasons for it: (1) The Scriptures say that Jesus first appeared to Mary Magdalene (Mark 16:9); and (2) the Blessed Mother did not require a strengthening of her faith as the apostles and others did.

Maximus the Confessor, in his book *The Life of the Virgin*, proposed that the Scriptures don't provide an account of this appearance because no one would believe it if the Mother claimed it; thus, Mary Magdalene had to become the first witness of the Resurrection.

Three popular biographies of Mary all suggest that Jesus appeared to her. Maximus the Confessor writes that Mary remained at the tomb, weeping and desiring to be near her Son. She witnessed the earthquake and the stone being rolled away. Maria of Agreda, in *The Mystical City of God*, recounts a version in which Jesus appears to Mary accompanied by the dead. Blessed Anne Catherine Emmerich details similar experiences of Mary and the consolation she received when seeing her Son risen from the dead.

The Church does not pray the Angelus during the Easter season. Instead, we pray the Regina Caeli (Queen of Heaven), which contemplates Mary's joy at the Resurrection. According to legend, Pope Gregory (whether Gregory the Great or Gregory the Fifth is disputed), while in a liturgical procession, heard the angels chanting "Regina Caeli." He thought it fitting to add the phrase "Pray for us to God" and make it a chant and prayer of the Church. Throughout Holy Week, we considered the sorrow of Mary as she walked with Christ and stood at the foot of the Cross. Now, for fifty days, we can consider her joy over seeing Jesus and knowing that He lives!

*Queen of Heaven, rejoice, alleluia.*
*He whom you merited to bear, alleluia.*
*Has risen, as He said, alleluia.*
*Pray for us to God, alleluia.*

*V. Rejoice and be glad, O Virgin Mary, alleluia.*
*R. For the Lord has truly risen, alleluia.*

*Let us pray. O God, who through the Resurrection*
*of Your Son Jesus Christ gave rejoicing to the world,*
*grant, we pray, that through His Mother, the Virgin*
*Mary, we may obtain the joy of everlasting life.*
*Through Christ our Lord. Amen.*

## Lenten Action

Memorize the Regina Caeli, and pray it at least once a day during the Easter season. If you like singing, listen to a chanted version online and learn it (visit, for example, https://www.youtube.com/watch?v=O8W4351sW14).

Monday of the Octave of Easter

# Faith That God Exists

*Have great confidence; God is always our
Father, even when He sends us trials.*

—Mother Directress to St. Faustina, *Diary,* par. 24

Many people do not believe in God. Some believe that the Scriptures are mere fantasy. Others reject every aspect of the Faith: the Trinity, Scripture, prayer, redemption, and so forth. Our Lenten journey, culminating with Easter Sunday, should assure us of God's existence and that He created the world. And in the fullness of time, He sent Jesus to be born of the Virgin and to die on the Cross, only to defeat death by rising from the dead. This Lenten experience with Our Lady's apparitions should reinforce our belief in God. Throughout the centuries, those to whom Our Lady appeared, young and old alike, shared their stories and the messages they received. These visionaries held on to their belief in what they experienced. Their stories reinforce what we already know and believe.

And our faith is reinforced not only by apparitions of Our Lady, but also by apparitions of Jesus Himself. One of the most famous apparitions occurred in the twentieth century, received by St. Faustina Kowalska in Poland. Jesus came to her and spoke about the vastness of His Divine Mercy.

Some people might be inclined to doubt that Jesus existed or that He was God. Some people begin to doubt or even deny God because of trials or bad experiences they face. Hopefully, as we consider the words of Jesus this week, they will reinforce for us the truth of His existence and His love for us. We have so many reminders of God's existence: creation, answered prayers, examples of providence, miracles both big and small, and much more.

It's easy for us to doubt God, especially when He seems distant and uninvolved in our lives. In those moments, let us foster greater faith in His existence by calling to mind those reminders of His loving presence in our lives.

*Jesus, I place my trust in You, and I am grateful for the many things that assure me that You exist and love me very much.*

### Easter Action

Look for the small events today that remind you that God exists. Then say a prayer of thanksgiving.

# Trust That God Loves You

*God will not deny His mercy to anyone. Heaven and earth
may change, but God's mercy will never be exhausted.*

—St. Faustina, *Diary*, par. 72

Some people go through life without being told they are loved
by the most important people in their lives. Even worse, they
might be told that they are not loved and begin to believe that.
This can affect how a person relates to God and receives His
love. If a person was raised by an abusive father, he may struggle
with relating to God as a Father. If a person was told that she is
unlovable, she might doubt that God could love her.

St. John reminds us in his Gospel that "God so loved the
world that he gave his only Son" (John 3:16). God loved us so
much that He sent Jesus, the Word made flesh, to live our life,
to redeem every aspect of our humanity, and ultimately to die
on the Cross for our salvation. In His love for the wandering
Israelites, God sent them manna from heaven. Jesus loves us
so much that He left us the Eucharist so that He could remain
with us on earth until the end of time. His love is so great that
it could not be contained by the grave, and He rose from the
dead so that we might have eternal life.

Our Holy Week experience was one of love. Jesus washed the feet of His disciples. He died on the Cross. He conquered the grave. When you need to be reminded of God's love for you, look at a crucifix and remind yourself that Jesus did this for you. Jesus died for you. You are loved by the God of the universe, the Savior of the world.

*Jesus, deepen my trust in your love for me.*

## Easter Action

Take a crucifix into your hands, and look at what Jesus did for you. Repeat the words "Jesus, I know You love me" several times. Then profess your love for Jesus in your own words.

Wednesday of the Octave of Easter

# Trust That God Forgives You

*My daughter, tell the whole world about My inconceivable mercy. I desire that the Feast of Mercy be a refuge and shelter for all souls, and especially for poor sinners. On that day the very depths of My tender mercy are open. I pour out a whole ocean of graces upon those souls who approach the Fount of My Mercy. The soul that will go to Confession and receive Holy Communion shall obtain complete forgiveness of sins and punishment. On that day all the divine floodgates through which graces flow are opened.*

—Jesus to St. Faustina, *Diary*, par. 699

We have all done things of which we are not proud. St. Paul reminds us that all have sinned and fallen short of the glory of God (see Rom. 3:23). Fortunately, Jesus gave the apostles authority to forgive sins. That happens through the sacrament of Reconciliation. During our Lenten journey, we examined our consciences and made a decision to receive the sacrament, as many people do during Lent. After we confess our sins and express our sorrow, we hear those words of absolution: "I absolve you from your sins." Those words give us much comfort. We hear that we are forgiven. Jesus, in the person of the priest, forgives us.

Many people, after celebrating the sacrament, remark that they feel a sense of relief and the heaviness of sin lifted from them. Yet, even though we hear the words of absolution, we could wonder: *Did God really forgive me?* The Scriptures are filled with examples of people who were given second chances. Even Peter, after denying Jesus, renewed his love three times after the Resurrection (see John 21:15–17). Many saints were grievous sinners, but they had an experience of God's love and mercy and became the saints they are today. We are sinners with a future as saints. If you doubt God's forgiveness, pray for greater trust in His mercy. Maybe it's time to go to Confession again and hear those words once more, so that we might believe they are true for us.

*Jesus, give me a greater trust in Your love, mercy, and forgiveness.*

### Easter Action

What is your practice of Confession like? Twice a year? Consider making more frequent confessions — once a month, once every few months. When you do, you will foster a greater trust in God's forgiveness, because you will know and believe you are forgiven.

Thursday of the Octave of Easter

# Trust That God Hears Your Prayers

*When I steeped myself in prayer, I was transported in spirit to the chapel, where I saw the Lord Jesus, exposed in the monstrance. In place of the monstrance, I saw the glorious face of the Lord, and He said to me,* **What you see in reality, these souls see through faith. Oh, how pleasing to me is their great faith! You see, although there appears to be no trace of life in Me, in reality it is present in its fullness in each and every Host. But for me to be able to act upon a soul, the soul must have faith. O how pleasing to Me is living faith!**

—Jesus to St. Faustina, *Diary*, par. 1420

When you pray, do you believe that God hears you and cares about you? We sometimes doubt that He does. That doubt might occur when what we pray for is not granted. We pray for healing, and someone dies. We pray for peace, and there is war. We pray for clarity, and there is confusion. Such experiences easily lead to doubting that our prayers matter.

Jesus taught in the Scriptures, "Ask and you shall receive" (see Matt. 7:7). Jesus wants us to ask. He wants us to make petitions. When He taught the Our Father to the apostles, He included different intentions: "Thy kingdom come, Thy will be done ...

forgive us." Our petitionary prayer invites us to a greater trust in God's will for our lives and the lives of others.

The saints prayed with great confidence in God. St. Philip Neri prayed for an intense experience of the Holy Spirit, and his heart literally expanded. St. Clare of Assisi, taking the monstrance, prayed and repelled the enemies who wanted to overtake her convent. We should pray with the same conviction. And in those moments when we doubt the efficacy of prayer, it is an invitation for us to remember all that God has done. Remember the answered prayers of your life. And have trust and confidence that God will continue to answer your prayers throughout your life.

*Jesus, give me a greater trust that You hear and answer my prayers.*

## Easter Action

Be persistent in your petitionary prayer. Do not give up.

Friday of the Octave of Easter

# Faith in Eternal Life

*My superiors sent me to the novitiate in Cracow. An inconceivable*
*joy reigned in my soul. When we arrived at the novitiate, Sister*
*Henry was dying. A few days later she came to me [in spirit, after her*
*death] and bid me to go to the Mother Directress of Novices [Sister*
*Margaret] and tell her to ask her confessor, Father Rospond, to offer*
*one Mass for her and three ejaculatory prayers. At first I agreed, but*
*the next day I decided I would not go to Mother Directress, because I*
*was not sure whether this had happened in a dream or in reality. And*
*so I did not go. The following night the same thing was repeated more*
*clearly; I had no more doubt. Still, in the morning, I decided not to*
*tell the Directress about it unless I saw her [Sister Henry] during the*
*day. At once I ran into her in the corridor. She reproached me for*
*not having gone immediately, and a great uneasiness filled my soul.*
*So I went immediately to Mother Directress and told her everything*
*that had happened to me. Mother responded that she would take*
*care of the matter. At once peace reigned in my soul, and on the*
*third day this sister came to me and said, "May God repay you."*

—St. Faustina, *Diary*, par. 21


For several months I journeyed with a young husband, his wife,
and their children through the man's terminal cancer. I had the
opportunity to be with him and his family the night before he

died. It was a grace-filled evening of prayer. Every Hail Mary called to mind the fact that Mary was soon going to pray for him at the hour of his death. Every Fatima Prayer and the words "lead all souls to heaven" became tangible because that was our prayer for him.

The next morning, I received the news that he had died. I returned to the hospital and consoled the man's wife, parents, and brothers. One of his brothers told me of the death, saying that the man cried out, "I think I'm dying; I think I'm dying." And a few moments later, he said the name of Jesus, closed his eyes, and transitioned from this life to the one Jesus promises.

*Jesus.* Why did he say the name of our Savior? I cannot help but believe it was because he saw the Lord face-to-face. The one in whom he believed now greeted him in eternal life. That story not only encouraged his family but also helped me during that experience. I believe the story reinforces for us our faith in eternal life.

When someone dies, it is easy to wonder whether and even doubt that we will see that person again—to wonder whether Heaven is real. The story of that father reminds me often of the heavenly paradise we hope to enter one day. It gives me faith in eternal life and confidence that we will see our loved ones again. We must hold on to our faith and hope and deepen our faith in eternal life.

*Jesus, give me a greater faith that one day I will live in Your presence.*

### Easter Action

Visit a cemetery and remind yourself that the grave will not have the final word.

Saturday of the Octave of Easter

# Faith in the Real Presence

*I find myself so weak that were it not for Holy Communion
I would fall continually. One thing alone sustains me, and
that is Holy Communion. From it I draw my strength; in it
is all my comfort. I fear life on days when I do not receive
Holy Communion. I fear my own self. Jesus concealed in
the Host is everything to me. From the tabernacle I draw
strength, power, courage and light. Here, I seek consolation
in time of anguish. I would not know how to give glory
to God if I did not have the Eucharist in my heart.*

—St. Faustina, *Diary*, par. 1037

In every chapel of the Daughters of St. Paul, these words are
etched in the wall near the tabernacle: "Do Not Fear. I am with
You. From Here I want to enlighten. Live with a penitent heart."
Every time a sister visits the Blessed Sacrament and prays in the
chapel, she is reminded of these words. But these words are also
meant for us.

In our lives, we will face difficult situations and become overwhelmed. And where do we turn? It's easy to try to self-medicate
by working more or using alcohol or turning to some other outlet.
As a believer, the right answer is to run to the tabernacle, to lay

before the Lord Jesus our fears and anxieties, the joys and the sorrows of our lives. Going before the tabernacle reminds us that God is with us. That we have nothing to fear. And when we sit before the Blessed Sacrament, Jesus wishes to inspire us. He speaks subtly.

The Gospel teaches us about the Eucharist. Jesus tells us that He is the Bread of Life and that whoever eats His Body and drinks His Blood will have eternal life. He took bread on the night of the Last Supper and said, "This is my Body," and a chalice of wine and said, "This is my Blood." At times, we might doubt the Real Presence of Jesus in the Blessed Sacrament. At those moments, we must foster a deeper faith in this reality, and we can pray, "I believe; help my unbelief." If you struggle with doubt that Jesus is present in the Blessed Sacrament, spend some time before the tabernacle or before a monstrance, and ask Him to reveal Himself to you. It is there that Jesus is with us and wants to enlighten us.

*Lord Jesus, present in all the tabernacles of the world, give me greater faith in Your Real Presence.*

## Easter Action

When you drive by a Catholic church, make the Sign of the Cross, calling to mind Christ's Presence. Better yet, stop by, and if the door is open, spend a few moments with the Savior.

Divine Mercy Sunday

# Trust in God's Promises

*Oh, how great is God's generosity! Blessed be*
*the Lord, who is faithful in His promises.*

—St. Faustina, *Diary*, par. 1300

When Jesus taught during His public ministry, He made many promises. He said, "Come to me all you who labor and are burdened, and I will give you rest" (Matt. 11:28). The Beatitudes offer many promises: that the poor will inherit the kingdom; that the merciful will receive mercy; that those who mourn will be comforted. Regarding the Eucharist, Jesus promises eternal life. These promises provide hope.

This week's focus has been on faith and trust. We often have doubts. We might doubt the promises of Jesus, either intellectually, not believing they could be true, or even experientially, saying, "I have mourned but was not comforted," or "I've shown mercy, but mercy has not been shown in return." We need to maintain our trust that God keeps His promises.

The celebration of Divine Mercy reminds us of all the promises that Jesus spoke to St. Faustina regarding His merciful love. Jesus promises that the floodgates of mercy are open on this day and that the Chaplet of Divine Mercy is efficacious when prayed with the dying. If you haven't read St. Faustina's *Diary*, I encourage you to do so; in it you will discover Jesus' promises for you. If the *Diary* is too dense, consider Susan Tassone's book *Day by Day with St. Faustina*.

*Jesus I trust in Your promises for me.*

## Easter Action

Pray the Divine Mercy Chaplet, and at the end, repeat the words "Jesus, I trust in You!"

# Conclusion

You meet lots of people when you go on a pilgrimage, especially if you go with a group. These people become friends for a time, and you might stay in touch with them for a while. I remember my first pilgrimage in 2005 as a sixteen-year-old. I remember many of the people and our experiences together, but unfortunately, we didn't stay in communication. I often wonder about those people. I think about the thief whom I had dinner with in Lourdes, and whether he is in jail or if he found a job and is providing for his family. And then there is Anna, whom I met on the last day of my 2018 Lourdes visit and whose story introduced this book and provided the format for our Lenten journey.

As I have given talks throughout the country about the Blessed Mother, I often weave in Anna's story about pilgrimage, because I believe it to be a powerful testament of her faith and trust in God. When I was writing this book, I wanted to reconnect with Anna. I knew her name, where she lived, and the kind of job she had, but I had no contact information. I searched for her online and found she had no social media presence. I wanted to reach out to her and get her permission to tell her story anonymously in the beginning of this book. I entrusted this wish to divine providence.

In the spring of 2019, the relics of St. John Vianney traveled throughout the country, visiting various cathedrals, churches, and shrines. I missed the Wisconsin date due to a traveling commitment, but I saw that the relics would visit Marytown in Illinois. I decided to make the three-hour (one-way) pilgrimage to pray before the saintly priest of Ars. I arrived around three o'clock and decided I'd stay until around six o'clock. As the time came for me to leave, I looked at the line and thought I recognized someone. Immediately I thought: "That's Anna from Lourdes." By the time I started to look for her, she had left the line and moved somewhere else in the chapel. I eventually found her, and once she saw me, she remembered that I was the priest from Lourdes. I shared with her that I told her story in talks I gave and was writing a book and wanted to include her story in it. She gave me permission. She went on to tell me that she related the story of my dinner with the thief to lots of people.

I had the opportunity to inquire further of Anna about the rest of her pilgrimage. She shared about going to Poland and how she made the Spiritual Exercises of St. Ignatius of Loyola in Spain, which was an unexpected surprise for her. During the Spiritual Exercises, a person prays for several hours a day with the Scriptures. In God's word, the Trinity speaks and enlightens. Anna's pilgrimage was a starting point in the process of conversion, forgiveness, healing, and developing trust. Each and every day, she must decide to pray and follow, to forgive and heal. A pilgrimage is only a beginning of what is left to come. It provides us with strength on our journey through life.

# Conclusion

This is the end of our Lenten and Divine Mercy spiritual pilgrimage. Having listened to our Mother and the Savior, we can now live the fruit of our pilgrimage each and every day until we arrive at the gates of the Kingdom of Heaven.

# Acknowledgments

Donna-Marie Cooper O'Boyle inspired me to write this book. I read her book *Advent with Our Lady of Fatima* in 2018 as a way to prepare my heart for Christmas. As I made my way through the book, I thought that it would be nice if Sophia Institute Press had a similar book for Lent. I wrote to John Barger, who agreed. I'd like to thank John for his patience with me, because I am often delayed in my writing projects due to my work as a parish priest.

Special thanks to Nancy Lind, a seasonal parishioner of mine, who is a professor at an Illinois university and editor of many books in her discipline. She graciously looked over my manuscript, correcting the errors I did not have time to review, and provided suggestions where content was lacking.

Thank you to Michael O'Neil, Relevant Radio host, popularly known as "the Miracle Hunter," who provided invaluable consultative feedback on apparitions I should include or not include as part of my daily reflections.

Special thanks to John O'Brien, a faithful follower of mine on Twitter. When I requested help in finding quotes from the diary of St. Faustina, because I couldn't find my copy, he stepped up to the plate and delivered. His assistance was invaluable to me.

In 2018, when I met Anna, I knew that her story would influence a lot of my preaching, speaking, and perhaps even writing. I was grateful to have the opportunity to reconnect with her stateside and learn more about her pilgrimage. Her story also inspired the format of this book, as indicated in the introduction.

This was one of the most difficult books I have written. In fact, I wanted to give up and not write it. I'd like to thank those who encouraged me to keep writing, especially Nancy Lind, Penny Paye Price, Jessica Marchant, and the many others with whom I shared about this writing project, who also encouraged me and cheered me on to the finish line. When I wanted to give up, I always heard in the back of mind the voice of my best-selling author friend Susan Tassone, who kept telling me how invaluable this book would be. Thank you to all who encouraged me.

# About the Author

Fr. Edward Looney was ordained a priest for the Diocese of Green Bay in June 2015 and is an internationally recognized Marian theologian, writer, speaker, and radio personality. He is a member of the Mariological Society of America and was elected by his peers to serve on the administrative council in 2016. He is the best-selling author of *A Heart Like Mary's* (Ave Maria Press), *A Rosary Litany* (Our Sunday Visitor), and *Our Lady of Good Help: A Prayer Book for Pilgrims* (TAN Books). His writings appear in *Catholic Digest* and online at *Catholic Exchange* and Aleteia, and he hosts the podcast *How They Love Mary*. Fr. Looney serves two rural Wisconsin parishes. You can follow him on social media: @FrEdwardLooney.

# Sophia Institute

Sophia Institute is a nonprofit institution that seeks to nurture the spiritual, moral, and cultural life of souls and to spread the Gospel of Christ in conformity with the authentic teachings of the Roman Catholic Church.

Sophia Institute Press fulfills this mission by offering translations, reprints, and new publications that afford readers a rich source of the enduring wisdom of mankind.

Sophia Institute also operates the popular online resource CatholicExchange.com. *Catholic Exchange* provides world news from a Catholic perspective as well as daily devotionals and articles that will help readers to grow in holiness and live a life consistent with the teachings of the Church.

In 2013, Sophia Institute launched Sophia Institute for Teachers to renew and rebuild Catholic culture through service to Catholic education. With the goal of nurturing the spiritual, moral, and cultural life of souls, and an abiding respect for the role and work of teachers, we strive to provide materials and programs that are at once enlightening to the mind and ennobling to the heart; faithful and complete, as well as useful and practical.

Sophia Institute gratefully recognizes the Solidarity Association for preserving and encouraging the growth of our apostolate over the course of many years. Without their generous and timely support, this book would not be in your hands.

www.SophiaInstitute.com
www.CatholicExchange.com
www.SophiaInstituteforTeachers.org

Sophia Institute Press® is a registered trademark of Sophia Institute. Sophia Institute is a tax-exempt institution as defined by the Internal Revenue Code, Section 501(c)(3). Tax ID 22-2548708.